The Oedipus Legend

The tragic story of King Oedipus is one of the great dramas that we have inherited from ancient Greece. It has penetrated the literature, legend, and language of all ages.

Towering above the gallery of characters that Sophocles created are two who stand as universal symbols of human nature in all its frailty and strength: Oedipus, the king who unknowingly killed his father and married his mother and who atoned for these crimes by a voluntary act of self-punishment . . . and Antigone, his daughter, who placed justice and dignity above her own life.

Paul Roche has revised his classic 1958 translation, rendering the Theban plays into a contemporary English that brings the characters and story to life with all the power, clarity, and emotion of the original Greek.

PAUL ROCHE is a distinguished poet and translator. In addition to *The Oedipus Plays of Sophocles*, his translations include *The Orestes Plays of Aeschylus, The Bible's Greatest Stories*, and the works of Sappho.

THE OEDIPUS PLAYS OF
Sophocles

OEDIPUS THE KING
OEDIPUS AT COLONUS
ANTIGONE

A newly revised

and updated translation by

Paul Roche

A PLUME BOOK

PLUME
Published by the Penguin Group
Penguin Group (USA) Inc., 375 Hudson Street, New York, New York 10014, U.S.A.
Penguin Group (Canada), 10 Alcorn Avenue, Toronto,
Ontario, Canada M4V 3B2 (a division of Pearson Penguin Canada Inc.)
Penguin Books Ltd., 80 Strand, London WC2R 0RL, England
Penguin Ireland, 25 St. Stephen's Green, Dublin 2, Ireland
(a division of Penguin Books Ltd.)
Penguin Group (Australia), 250 Camberwell Road, Camberwell,
Victoria 3124, Australia (a division of Pearson Australia Group Pty. Ltd.)
Penguin Books India Pvt. Ltd., 11 Community Centre, Panchsheel Park,
New Delhi – 110 017, India
Penguin Books (NZ), Cnr Airborne and Rosedale Roads, Albany, Auckland,
New Zealand (a division of Pearson New Zealand Ltd.)
Penguin Books (South Africa) (Pty.) Ltd., 24 Sturdee Avenue, Rosebank,
Johannesburg 2196, South Africa

Penguin Books Ltd., Registered Offices: 80 Strand, London WC2R 0RL, England

Published by Plume, a member of Penguin Group (USA) Inc.
Previously published in a Mentor edition.

First Meridian Printing, May 1996
First Plume Printing, September 2004
20 19 18

Copyright © Paul Roche, 1958, 1991
Copyright renewed Paul Roche, 1986
All rights reserved

 REGISTERED TRADEMARK—MARCA REGISTRADA

Library of Congress Card No. 91-61300

Printed in the United States of America

ΣΟΦΟΚΛΕΟΥΣ ΑΝΤΙΓΟΝΗ

Ω ΚΟΙΝΟΝ ΑΥΤΑΔΕΛΦΟΝ ΙΣΜΗΝΗΣ ΚΑΡΑ
ΑΡΟΙΣΘΟΤΙ ΖΕΥΣ ΤΩ ΝΑΠΟΙΔΙΠΟΥ ΚΑΚΩΝ
ΟΠΟΙΟΝ ΟΥΧΙ ΝΩ Ν ΕΤΙ ΖΩΣΑΙΝ ΤΕΛΕΙ
ΟΥΔΕΝ ΓΑΡ ΟΥΤ ΑΛΓΕΙΝΟΝ ΟΥΤΑΤΗΣ ΑΤΕΡ
ΟΥΤ ΑΙΣΧΡΟΝ ΟΥΤ ΑΤΙΜΟΝ ΕΣΘΟΠΟΙΟΝ ΟΥ
ΤΩΝ ΣΩΝ ΤΕ ΚΑΜΩΝ ΟΥΚ ΟΠΩΠ ΕΓΩ ΚΑΚΩΝ

Contents

Foreword

THE GREAT ENCOUNTER

Sophocles, who died at the age of well over ninety, two thousand three hundred and ninety-seven years ago, was one of the world's greatest poets and dramatists, and he speaks to us today with a message no less necessary and elevating than it was to the Greeks of the fifth century B.C. We too need to be told that man is but a limited and contingent creature, subject to sudden disrupting forces. Success is not finally to be measured by fame or material prosperity. Human greatness consists ultimately in nobly accepting the responsibility of being what we are; human freedom, in the personal working out of our fate in terms appropriate to ourselves. Though we may be innocent, we are all potentially guilty, because of the germ of self-sufficiency and arrogance in our nature. We must remember always that we are only man and be modest in our own conceits. Our place in the total pattern of the cosmos is only finite. That is not to say that it may not be glorious. Whatever our circumstances, we can achieve and endure through to essential greatness. It is not what fate has in store for us that matters, but what we do with it when it comes. There may be suffering, but no abiding hopelessness. No power, no imposition, no catastrophe, can uproot the personal dignity of each human being. The seeming caprice and unfairness of life, striking some down and pampering others, is only the beginning of the Great Encounter. Both the choice and the destiny are ours.

—Paul Roche

Soller,
Majorca,
1991

Introduction

THE THEBAN TRILOGY

The story of Oedipus King of Thebes, his success, his fall, his awed and hallowed end—in brief, the Theban Legend—was already old in the time of Sophocles. Perhaps it stood to the great poet and dramatist in something of the same light that the legend of King Arthur and the Holy Grail stood to the poet Tennyson: a legend celebrated by several hundred years of song and poetry.

But, whereas Tennyson looked back on a dreamlike world of chivalry, and helped to sustain the dream of courtly romance, Sophocles looked back on an elemental world of human frailty, pride, and punishment, and helped to sustain the dreadful inevitability of a family moving toward catastrophe. The world of King Arthur seemed beautifully impossible and Tennyson left it so; the world of King Oedipus seemed thankfully improbable but Sophocles left it terrifyingly possible.

In each of the three plays that comprise his Theban Trilogy—*Oedipus the King, Oedipus at Colonus*, and the *Antigone*—Sophocles shows us a character pursued to and pursuing its end amid the full illusion both of freedom and of destiny and so to a gloriously headstrong doom. It is true that the downfall of the House of Oedipus was foretold by the gods even before Oedipus was born, but it was foretold because it was going to happen; it was not going to happen because it was foretold.

The tragedy of King Oedipus was not only that he suffered the improbabilities of murdering his father and marrying his mother—both were mistakes anyway—the tragedy was that having murdered his father and married his mother he made the fully responsible mistake of finding it out. As he was an upright man, but proud, the

gods allowed him to make the first mistake; as he was a
headstrong man, but overweening in self-confidence, he
allowed himself to make the second. Zeal mysteriously
worked with destiny to trip him up on his self-righteous-
ness and then reveal an arrogance which pressed forward
to calamity.

But even fallen pride need not remain prostrate. In
the second play, the *Oedipus at Colonus,* we are shown
an old man, blinded, beaten, hunted through the years,
rise to a new dignity by the very fact of his being the
recognized vehicle of divine justice. We now know the
worst that can happen to man, but it can only happen
through a foolish stepping outside from the stream of
man's right relationship to God. Now we see Oedipus,
by his magnanimous acceptance of Fate, step back again.
He is both cursed and blessed, and a living testimony to
the vindication of man through suffering: not of course
suffering in the Christian sense—for the horror and recal-
citrance are still there—but suffering in that it is a lesson,
a proud and acknowledged testimony to the truth.

In the last play, the *Antigone,* Sophocles returns to the
theme of the first and shows us again what happens when
the ostensibly good man succumbs to pride. This time,
however, there is an added poignancy: Creon, who is the
protagonist rather than Antigone, and who is a kind of
second Oedipus in his ruthless pursuit of what he thinks
is right, brings final ruin to the House of Oedipus,
destroying not only himself, his wife, his son, the love
of these for him, but the very person his son is going to
marry and the one who is most dedicated to the right—
Antigone.

So must always be the end of man without God, even
religious man—for both Oedipus and Creon thought that
they were religious. The horror for us, as it was for the
Greeks, is precisely to see that an Oedipus or a Creon
can so easily be ourselves. Both display the glory and
the weakness (the fatal flaw) of self-sufficient man. And
when Oedipus, the once upright, is dragged piecemeal,

by his own doing, from wealth and power, is stripped of reputation, made to wallow in a bed of murder, incest, suicide, even personal disfigurement, the audience passes through such territories of fear and pity that the human heart is altogether purged.

THE RE-CREATION

If it is true that dramatic poetry is the language of speech, but speech made perfect, and true that poetry gives to plot its feeling, then my aim in this new translation of Sophocles is to make that speech as real as possible without ever letting it cease to be poetry. The difficulty of doing this for Sophocles is that he was no ordinary poetic genius. All great poets can rise to an occasion; but Sophocles does not need an occasion: he achieves his magical effects at will. He makes the simplest words and phrases sound like the loftiest epic utterance, and he makes the loftiest epic utterance sound as natural as everyday speech. With Sophocles, dramatic poetry is the language of speech made perfect and the perfection of language made speech.

Herein lies the challenge to the translator: after he has captured the sense of that perfect speech, how does he proceed to capture the magic of its sound? For if poetry lies somewhere between meaning and music, sense and sound, it is obvious that when meanings cross the barrier of different tongues they do not take their music with them: they have to assume new sounds and these new sounds may not be the aesthetic equivalent of the original. This is true of any two languages. "La plume de ma tante" is obviously not the same as "My aunt's pen," though who shall say exactly where the difference lies?

We need not, however, go further than our own language to see that different sounds can have the same meaning and yet a quite dissimilar feeling. "Lamp" is not the aesthetic equivalent of "light," nor "daybreak" of "early morning." "Highroad" does not have the same feeling to it as "main road" nor "chair" as "seat." The differences here are subtle but they are there. Sometimes the differences are crude and obvious: no one (even in his cups) would get up from a meal saying, "Well, I've never had better cutlets of dead calf or swallowed mellower fermented grape juice."

It is, then, not merely differences of meaning that control differences of feeling, but also differences of sound. "Thou odoriferous stench, sound rottenness," is not at all the same as "You sweet smell, healthy decay," though who will say the meaning is different? "In Xanadu did Kubla Khan a stately pleasure dome decree" bears almost no emotional resemblance to, "Kubla Khan decided upon a fine fun dome in Xanadu." It is precisely these different values of sound that guide and indicate the changes of feeling in any language. It is the balance of sounds in an infinitely complex interplay of rhythms and cadences that creates all those shifting associations of meaning and feeling, those allusions, hints and half-meanings, that constitute the pattern of living speech.

This is what makes translating poetry so exacting. It is not merely meanings that a translator has to match but feelings, and for this there are no rules that he can follow—he can only depend upon his ear. And to do this he must be a poet. If he cannot tell that "my Italy" has not the same ring to it as "Italia mia," that "chez moi" is not quite the same as "home," and that "the alpha and the omega" is the same and yet utterly different from "A to Z," then he had better leave the business of translating poetry alone. He might possibly end up by rendering Tennyson's famous lines: "Break, break, break on thy cold grey stones, O sea" into "Cassez-vous, cassez-vous, cassez-vous sur vos froids gris cailloux O mer,"* which would be equivalent aesthetically to someone's translating the glorious cry of Xenophon's Ten Thousand: "Thalassa! Thalassa!" (The Sea! The Sea!) into "A vast expanse of salt water! A vast expanse of salt water!" Perfectly accurate of course.

*I am indebted to the late Miss Edith Hamilton for this witty example.

It does not do then in poetry to forget sound. All feeling is controlled by the shape of sounds—their differences of cadence and rhythm. It is not simply that different sounds have different meanings, but that the same meanings have different sounds. Words are unbelievably sensitive. And in poetry mere clarity has very little to do with feeling. An increase of clarity can even spell the end of feeling; for poetry being half music has the power of making itself felt long before it has made itself fully understood.

I fled him down the nights and down the days,
I fled him down the arches of the years . . .

can be made far more straightforward and clear (and valueless): "For many years I made great efforts to avoid him." The health has gone from it.

These things being so, I took it as my principle that the translator of poetry must never rest satisfied with simply rendering the correct meaning of the words. This is only half his duty. The other half is to search out and to organize from the paucity or the abundance of words in his own language those words which can conjure up a similar feeling. He must rework the original words into a new system of sounds and rhythms that are so true to the nuances of his own language that they might almost seem to have been first created in that language to express the original feelings. He must therefore be aware of the essential differences between his own language and the original and yet be able to see constant analogies between them. For it is only by relating the known to the less known that a transformation takes place. Recreation, not imitation, is what is called for.

Suppose, for instance, that the translator of Sophocles decides to cast his lines in hexameters simply because the Greek trimeter is also a six-measured line. He will find at once that he has not got the aesthetic equivalent: the Greek trimeter is light and quick, the English hexameter dawdles and hesitates.

Suppose he goes to the other extreme and far from

trying to imitate the Greek he ignores it and casts his lines in English rhymed tetrameter. He may get lightness and speed all right but now he will have something as foreign in feeling to the original as *The Rime of the Ancient Mariner* is to the Book of Job.

The poet-translator, then, must keep his eyes and ears on each of the languages: never imitating the one but seizing every chance for a parallel effect with the other. Compared to Anglo-Saxon poetry Greek poetry is spare in metaphor but rich in sound. He must somehow resolve this difference so that the Greek sparsity of ornament does not come out in English as bald uninspiring sound. Compared to Anglo-Saxon poetry Greek poetry is often direct and primitive in emotion but condenses great complexity of expression in a single compound epithet: the translator must somehow contrive to find a bond between the two so that the Greek compressed simplicity does not come out in English as verbiage or naïveté.

The style of Shakespeare and the style of the King James Bible (pillars of English literary form) could not be more different in sensibility from the style of Sophocles, and yet the poet-translator must find some analogy between them if he is to make a bridge between the two sensibilities. Luckily, there *are* analogies, likenesses, parallel feelings, for the design of words and the beauty of sound. The two languages do in fact pay attention to a great many of the same things: there is a preoccupation with cadence, which shows itself in a love of alliteration and assonance and the associative power of similar sound; there is an attention to rhythm, which shows itself in (among other things) the well-timed pause, the break in the middle of the line; a love of antithesis of sound and sense: there is a feeling for the symmetrical phrase as well as the asymmetrical as a means to emphasis; the use of repetition and parallelisms of speech for pointing up a phrase or creating pathos; a predilection for twists of expression, telling paradoxes, oxymora, litotes, and a whole host of figures of speech that help to put salt on the tongue and tonic in the head. These are the powerful emotive devices that Greek shares with Anglo-Saxon. If a translator is deaf to them in the Greek he will be deaf to them in English and he will remain comparatively numb to the feelings they engender. It is just here, it seems to me, that the poet-translator has his chance of paralleling the force and beauty of the Greek without ever deserting the native genius of English. He will be respecting similarities without at the same time attempting to camouflage differences.

In my own efforts I have been careful to watch Sophocles. Where he has repeated a word, I have repeated it; where he is rich in assonance and alliteration, I try to be; where he is harsh and staccato, I try to catch it; where he has a ringing tone, I try to ring.* I have tried to walk and to run, to rise and to sit, with the Master, but never by imitation, only by analogy, transposition, re-creation. In translation there has to be a change of instruments, but the tune, the feelings as relayed through sound, must remain as quiet, as excited, as sublime, as intense, as in the original.

Such is the challenge. The poet-translator has as his ideal the creation of a pattern of sound which gets so close to the feeling of the original that it goes beneath the barrier of language and time, and lays bare the original creations of the Master. We ought not to have to remind ourselves that Oedipus, Antigone, Creon, Jocasta, and the other characters of Sophoclean tragedy were first conceived as human beings. They have not changed since. They are in fact universal and timeless and we ought primarily to see them that way rather than as Greek characters in a Greek period piece.

The language of Sophocles is concentrated, vivid, spirited, and powerful. Cardinal Newman calls it, "the sweet composure, the melodious fullness, the majesty and grace of Sophocles." But it was also free, molten, fusile with elements taken from the lofty poetry of the epic, the strains of the lyric, and the lowly commonplaces of

---

*The reverse of this, of course, is not necessarily true: if I have repeated a word, it may not always be that Sophocles has repeated it.

the market square.* He was a careful craftsman but far from being a safety-first artist. Amazing agility and subtlety often consort with a quite conscious want of accuracy. He wrote in a Greek never quite heard before. He took risks with the language: coining words, inventing grammatical and syntactical constructions, condensing, eliding, twisting figures of speech inside out, and sometimes stretching the elasticity of the Greek language (that most lively of languages) to breaking point. But in the end, at least when it is given to the ear and not the eye alone to judge, he makes everything sound moderate, simple, and natural. In my efforts to follow him I have not scrupled to turn my back on the purely literary, the pedantic, and the circumspect in diction. I have used a language which I hope is contemporary but new, transcending if possible the mere aptness of a modern idiom. I daresay I have sometimes run the risk of looking "not quite right," but perhaps not more so than Sophocles himself might have looked to some of his contemporaries had they only seen his lines and never heard them. I have coined a construction here and there and, in the *Antigone,* a word, but always with only one end in view: a deepening of the fear, the pity, the love, the pathos, the hate, contained in the original. I have throughout thought more of the sequence of Sophocles' feelings and ideas than of the apparent grammatical connection of his words; remembering that Sophocles himself wrote at a time when the Greek language had not finally set. I have always asked myself not: is such and such a phrase rendered metaphrastically according to the book of grammar or, for that matter, according to the lexicon, but—is it true? Is it natural? Is it poetical and rhythmical? Is it dramatically convincing and expressive of the human heart?*

The choruses in Sophocles are swift, energetic, and

*There are echoes in Sophocles of the proverb, the cliché and (as far as we can tell) the colloquial phrase. I have not ostracized any of these where they have served dialogue and emotions.

*These are the questions that Lewis Campbell, one of the greatest Greek scholars of the last century, propounds to the would-be Sophoclean interpreter.

moving, but they are not easy. I have not tried to make them easy. I should hope, however, to have made them evocative. Their function in the original (helped on by dance, spectacle, and song) was to bridge the gap between the audience and the players and to intensify the emotion. For this reason I have allowed myself a very full vocabulary; for I wanted the widest possible range of sound. There seemed no reason, for instance, in avoiding the emotionally right word simply because it happened to be unusual or of non-Anglo-Saxon origin. There is a time for the simple and a time for the complex. The Sophoclean choruses in their tense and mobile harmony of shifting sounds had an effect more powerful than mere narration, more immediate than plot. There is a time for music and a time for reasoning.

The three plays that are given here are three of the only seven that have come down to us. Altogether, Sophocles wrote some hundred and twenty plays, but only a few fragments and the titles of some have survived. The last of the three in the Theban Trilogy, the *Antigone,* was written first and is sometimes said to be his thirty-second play in order of production. It probably belongs to his middle period and Sophocles must have been about fifty-five. The first of the three, *Oedipus the King,* was written some sixteen years later when Athens was at the height of her fame and power. The second play, *Oedipus at Colonus,* was written last—perhaps last of all his plays—when Sophocles was over ninety*: an old man well-loved and still distinguished for his refinement, balance, and nobility of mind, but perhaps a little disillusioned with life and ready to say good-bye to it. He had seen his sons rebel against him in court, and now was forced to see his darling Athens nearing the end of her death struggles with Sparta—bankrupt, tottering in the dust, her sacred olive groves cut down, and her springing fountains dry.

---

*Sophocles was between ninety and ninety-five years old when he wrote it. The reason for the uncertainty is that his birth is conjectured as being between 499 and 496 B.C. He died in 406 B.C. The play was first produced in 401 B.C. by his son Iophon (also a playwright).

Oedipus at Colonus has all the marks of an old man's last creative impulse. Almost gone are the devastating blow-by-blow concisions and concussions of the *Oedipus the King*. The play in lesser hands could easily have deteriorated into a ramble. Instead, it builds. We have episodes which are lengthy and unexpected but finally convincing. Above all, we are treated to language that is miraculous. After some hundred and twenty plays, and having won the first prize between eighteen and twenty-four times, Sophocles' mastery of dramatic verse is supreme. The words are often so simple and ordinary that one wonders (as with late Shakespeare) where the poetry is coming from. But it comes. In an accumulation of swift gentle strokes (especially in the farewell and demise of Oedipus), the words move us in a way reminiscent of something out of the Old Testament, like the Book of Job.

As did Sophocles, I attempted the *Antigone* first, and though I have not his advantage of being able to put some thirty-four years between it and the *Oedipus at Colonus*, I have perhaps unwittingly reflected something of his advance as a poet from the wonderful, but less mature, artistry of the *Antigone* to the perfect smoothness, naturalness, and sublimity of *Oedipus at Colonus*. No one of course would dare to suggest that the Greek of the *Antigone*, so strong and so beautiful, is not already perfect, but Sophocles himself might have thought so. Indeed, there is a pregnant phrase quoted by Plutarch in which Sophocles described his own development by saying that "after working off the Aeschylean grandiloquence of his earlier style, and then the artificiality and crudity of his own style, he thirdly arrived at one which was *most expressive of character and most perfect.*"* Be that as it may, rough diamonds in any language have their own perfection and a too consistent sparkle can dim the eye to deeper beauties.

---

*ηθιώτατ και βέλτιστον. I have taken this observation from *The Style of Sophocles* by Professor F. R. Earp (Cambridge, 1944), to whom I am greatly indebted for his illuminating analysis.

OEDIPUS
THE KING

for Duncan Grant
still my choice and master spirit
of this age

THE CHARACTERS

OEDIPUS, King of Thebes

A PRIEST of Zeus

CREON, brother of Jocasta

CHORUS of Theban elders

TIRESIAS, a blind prophet

JOCASTA, wife of Oedipus

A MESSENGER from Corinth

An old SHEPHERD

A PALACE OFFICIAL

Palace Attendants and Servants

Citizens of Thebes

Antigone, Ismene, and a Boy

TIME AND SETTING

Some fifteen years previously, OEDIPUS, *then a young man, was told by the Oracle at Delphi that he was destined to murder his father and marry his mother. Shocked, he determines never to go back to Corinth, where he was brought up by the king and queen, who he thinks are his father and mother. His wanderings bring him eventually to the city of Thebes, where his real father and mother reign. However, on the way, he brawls with an old man in a carriage over right of way and in a fit of temper kills him. Arrived at Thebes, he finds the city in an uproar: the king,* LAIUS, *has gone on a mysterious journey and never returned, and a female monster, the Sphinx, has taken up her position on a rock outside Thebes and is strangling the inhabitants one by one for not being able to answer her riddle.* OEDIPUS *answers it and the Sphinx throws herself from her rock. The citizens, in gratitude, make* OEDIPUS *their king and he marries* JOCASTA, *their widowed queen. No one knows that* JOCASTA *is* OEDIPUS's *real mother and that the old man he killed on the road was* LAIUS, *his father. Nor do they know that these parents of his had tried to murder him as a baby (because of another dreadful oracle), and thought they had succeeded. There follow fifteen years of apparent prosperity: a sham prosperity cloaking corruption. The gods are disgusted. Thebes is struck by plague. The people of the city, led by their priests and elders, flock around the great and successful* OEDIPUS, *now in the prime of life and power. He saved them once: he can save them again. Here the play begins.*

It is midmorning outside the palace of OEDIPUS, *with Thebes in the background. There is the sound of prayer and lamentation; the air is full of incense. A procession of children, youths, and elders, all holding olive branches*

*wreathed in white wool, are marshaled by a priest onto
the palace steps and group themselves around the altar of
Zeus.* OEDIPUS *comes out of the palace. He signals for
silence.*

Oedipus the King

OEDIPUS

My children, scions of the ancient Cadmean line,
  what is the meaning of this thronging round my feet,
   this holding out of olive boughs all wreathed in woe?
The city droops with elegaic sound
  and hymns with palls of incense hang.
I come to see it with my eyes, no messenger's.
Yes, I whom men call Oedipus the Great.

[*He turns to the* PRIEST]

Speak, Elder, you are senior here.
Say what this pleading means,
  what frightens you, what you beseech.
Coldblooded would I be, to be unmoved
  by petitioners so pitiful.

PRIEST

King Oedipus, the sovereign of our land,
  you see here young and old clustered round the shrine.
Fledglings some, essaying flight,
  and some much weighted down
  (as I by age, the Presbyter of Zeus),
  and striplings some—ambassadors of youth.
In the market place sit others too
  at Pallas's double altar, garlanded to pray,
  and at the shrine
  where Ismenus breathes oracles of fire.

Oh, look upon the city, see the storm
  that batters down this city's prow in waves of blood:

5

The crops diseased, disease among the herds.
The ineffectual womb rotting with its fruit.
A fever-demon wastes the town
   and decimates with fire, stalking hated
   through the emptied house where Cadmus dwelled.
While poverty-stricken night grows fat
   on groans and elegies in Hades' halls.
We know you are no god, omnipotent with gods.
That is not why we throw ourselves before you here,
   these little suppliants and I.
It is because on life's unequal stage
   we see you as first of men and consummate
   atoner to the powers above.
For it was you,
   coming to the Cadmus capital,
Who disenthralled us from the Sphinx (her greedy dues):
   that ruthless sorceress who sang.
Not primed by us, not taught by hidden lore,
   but god-inspired, we so believe,
You raised us up again and made us sound.
So, Oedipus, you most respected king,
   we plead with you to find for us a cure:
Some answer breathed from heaven, perhaps,
   or even enlightenment from man.
For still we see the prowess of your well-proved mind,
   its tested buoyancy.

So, go, you best of men.
Raise up our city. Go, now on your guard.
Your old devotion celebrates you still
   as Defender of the State. You must not let
   your reign go down as one when men
   were resurrected once—and once relapsed.
Mend the city, make her safe.
You had good omens once. You did your work.
Be equal to your stature now.
If king of men (as king you are),
   then be it of a kingdom manned and not a desert.
Poop and battlement are wasted when
   all is nothing but waste of men.

OEDIPUS

This quest that throngs you here, poor needy children,
  is no new quest to me.
I know too well, you all are sick, yet sick,
  not one so sick as I.
Your pain is single, each to each, it does not breed.
Mine is treble anguish crying out
  for the city, for myself, for you.
It was no man asleep you woke—ah no!—
But one in bitter tears and one
  perplexed in thought, found wandering.
  Who clutched the only remedy that came:
  to send the son of Menoeceus, Creon—
  my own Jocasta's brother—
to the place Apollo haunts at Pythia
  to learn what act or covenant of mine
  could still redeem the state.

And now I wonder.
I count the days. His time is up.
He does not come. He should be here.
But when he comes—the instant he arrives—
  whatsoever he shall tell me from the god,
  that to the hilt I'll do—or I am damned.

PRIEST

Reassuring words indeed! And timely too,
  for look, they're signaling that Creon comes.

[CREON *is seen approaching in the distance*]

OEDIPUS

His eyes are bright. O great Apollo,
  bring him here effulgent with success!

PRIEST

Yes, success it is, I think.
See the laurel chaplets thick with berries on his head!

OEDIPUS

We shall know in a moment. He can hear us now.

[OEDIPUS *shouts to him*]

What news, royal brother?
What mandate, Son of Menoeceus, from the mouth of
the god?

[*Enter* CREON]

CREON

Favorable! I'd even say, if all goes well,
our wounds will issue into blessings.

OEDIPUS

Which means? . . . You leave me half in hope,
half buried in despair.

CREON

Do you want to hear it publicly, on the spot,
or shall we go inside?

OEDIPUS

Speak out to all. It's more for them than me,
though more my own than my own soul.

CREON

Very well, then. This is what the god has said,
The Prince Apollo openly enjoins on us
to sever from the body politic
a monstrous growth that battens there:
stop feeding that which festers.

OEDIPUS

By what purge? How diagnosed?

CREON

By banishment. Or blood for blood.
The city frets with someone's blood.

OEDIPUS

Whose? Is the unhappy man not named?

CREON

Laius, sire. Him we had as king
in days before you ruled.

OEDIPUS

So I've heard . . . A man I never saw.

CREON

A murdered man. And now clearly is required
the just blood of his assassins.   .

OEDIPUS

But where in the world are they? Oh where can one
begin
to search the long-lost traces of forgotten crime?

CREON

"Here," says the god. "Seek and you shall find.
Only that escapes which never was pursued."

OEDIPUS

Where did Laius meet his violent end?
At home? In the fields? In foreign parts?

CREON

He planned a pilgrimage, he said; and so left home,
never to come back again the way he went.

OEDIPUS

He went alone? No companions and no witnesses
who could furnish a report?

CREON

Dead. All done to death but one, who fled in panic,
and he tongue-tied save on a single point.

OEDIPUS

What point? Tell it. Clues breed clues
and we must snatch at straws.

CREON

Brigands, this man insists, attacked the King:
not one but many, and they cut him down.

OEDIPUS

No brigand would be so bold, unless . . .
. unless bought—right here—bought with bribes.

CREON

So we thought, but with Laius gone
we were sunk in miseries and no one stirred.

OEDIPUS

What miseries could ever let you leave unsolved
the death and downfall of a king?

CREON

Sire, it was the siren Sphinx of riddles
who sang us from the shadowed past
to what was sorely present.

OEDIPUS

Then I'll go back and drag that shadowed past to light.
Oh yes, the pious Apollo and your piety
  has set on foot a duty to the dead:
A search which you and I together will pursue.
My designs could not be suited more:
  to avenge the god and Thebes in a single blow.
Ah! Not for any far-flung friend,
  but by myself and for myself I'll break this plague.
For who knows, tomorrow this selfsame murderer
  may turn his bloody hands on me.
The cause of Laius therefore is my own.

So, rise up, Children, and be off.
Take your prayer boughs too.
Summon here the counselors of Thebes,
  and muster too the Cadmus clan.
I am resolute, and shall not stop
  till with Apollo's help all-blessed we emerge,
  or else we are lost—beyond all purge.

[OEDIPUS *goes into the palace followed by* CREON]

PRIEST

Children, rise.
The King has pledged us all our pleas
  and we have heard Apollo's voice.
Oh, may he bring salvation in his hands
  and deal a death to all disease.

[*The* PRIEST *disperses the suppliants. The* CHORUS *of Theban Elders enters*]

ODE OF ENTRY

[*The first ode opens with a hymn to Apollo, the god of victory and healing (known as Paean). Its stately dactylic measure, as the* CHORUS *moves toward the altar of Zeus, is bright with hope yet weighted with awe and uncertainty.*]

*Then as the Elders survey the sufferings of Thebes, the
rhythm changes into one of dismay, broken by the sad
lines of trochees and iambs. In the final strophe and antistrophe the Elders clinch their prayer for help on a note
of energy and determination.*]

Strophe I

What god-golden voice from the gold-studded shrine of
                                          the Pytho
          Comes to our glorious Thebes?
My spirit is tremulous, racked with its eagerness. Help
              Healer of Delos—Paean!
I am fainting with fear of what fate you will fashion me
                                          now,
          Or turn in the turning of time.
Speak to me, Oracle, child everlastingly sprung
          From Hope so goldenly. Come!

Antistrophe I

I call on you first, Zeus's daughter, immortal Athena.
          Then on your sister, earth's guardian,
Artemis ringed round with praises and throned in our
                                          square.
          Ah! And far-shooting Phoebus.
You three that are champions swift to deliver, appear!
          For if ever the fire of disaster
Reared on our city, you beat its affliction away.
          Defend and be near us today.

Strophe II

          Sorrows in a legion.
          Sorrows none can cipher.
          No shaft of wit or weapon
          For a people stricken.
          Shriveled soil and shrinking
          Wombs in childbirth shrieking.
          Soul after soul like fire

Beats, beats upward soaring
To the god of the setting sun.

Antistrophe II

A decimated city
Dying. And deadly the dead.
All lying uncried for. But crying
Matrons and mothers graying
At every altar praying,
Till the chiming sorrow of dirges
Is splintered by shouts of the paean:
Rescue! O golden daughter
Of Zeus's with your smile.

Strophe III

Muffle the wildfire Ares
Warring with copper-hot fever
Without clash of sword or shield.
Whirl him back homeward and headlong.
Plunge him down from our shores
Into Amphitrite's foaming
Lap or the unquiet grave
Of hissing Thracian seas.
For, oh, what night has spared us
He does at break of day.
Zeus you sovereign of thunder,
Shiver him with lightning.

Antistrophe III

Aureate champion Apollo,
Let us sing the song of your arrows
Shot from the bow of the sun;
While Artemis blazing with torches
Courses the Lycean mountains.
And you, O Theban Bacchus,
Wine blushed, xanthic crowned,
You smiling god of succor,

> Come all torchlit flaring,
> Come wheeling with your Maenads,
> Fall on the god that is godless.

[OEDIPUS *has entered*]

First Episode

OEDIPUS

You pray! Then listen:
What you pray for you can have—
   remission of these miseries and help
   if you'll hear my plan:
   a plan to stop the plague.
I speak of course as stranger to the story
   and stranger to the crime,
   being too late your latest citizen
And helpless, therefore, to track it very far
   unless you lend me clues.
Wherefore, I boldly challenge
   all you Thebans here with this:
Does any man among you know
   who killed Laius son of Labdacus?
Such a one I now command
   to tell me everything.

[*He waits for a reply*]

If self-incrimination keeps him silent,
   let him be assured
He need fear nothing worse than banishment
   and he can depart unharmed.

[*He pauses again*]

Perhaps one of you is aware
   the murderer was someone from some other land.
Let him not be shy to say it.
I shall heap rewards on him,
   besides my deepest blessing.

[*No one stirs*]

What, silent still?
If anyone is out to shield a guilty friend
 (or is it guilty self?),
He'd best listen to the penalties I plan.
That man, whoever that man be,
 I this country's reigning king
Shall sever from all fellowship of speech and shelter,
 sacrifice and sacrament,
Even ritual touch of water, in this realm.
Thrust out from every home,
 he'll be the very picture of that pestilence
 he brought upon our city,
As Apollo's word from Pythia has just revealed to me.
Yes, such an ally, nothing less,
 am I of both religion and the murdered man.

As to the killer, slipping off alone
 or with a band of men,
I now call down a life to fit a life
 dragged out in degradation.
And if I myself should prove myself
 to have him in my halls an intimate,
Then on myself I call down every curse I've just invoked.
See to it that every syllable I say is done.
For my sake, for the god Apollo, and for this land,
 so fruitless now and so cast off by heaven.
Why, even without a sanction so divine,
 how could you find it in you to neglect
 a monarch's death and not pursue
 this ending to the best of men?
Whose very scepter I hold in my hands as King;
His marriage bed my bed of seed,
 our children even shared with share of her
 had he been blessed with progeny—
Oh, blessed and not struck down by fate!

Such ties swear me to his side
 as if he were my father.
I shall not rest until I've tracked the hand
 that slew the son of Labdacus,

the son of Polydorus, heir to Cadmus in the line
of ancient Agenor.
And those who disobey
I'll ask the gods to curse
with fields that never sprout
and wombs that never flower,
And all the horrors of this present plague and worse.
The rest of you, my loyal men of Thebes,
who think with me, may Justice champion
and the whole of heaven help.

CHORUS

Great king, your oath will make a perjuror of me
if I do not tell the truth. I swear
I am not the killer, nor can I show you
who the killer is.
Apollo proposed the search, it's up to him
to point the culprit out.

OEDIPUS

Certainly, but show me a man who can force
the hand of heaven.

CHORUS

Then, the next best thing, if I may say it . . .

OEDIPUS

Next best, third best, say it—anything.

CHORUS

My lord, there lives a man who with a king's eyes sees
the secrets of a king: Tiresias of Apollo.
He is our source of light, our chance of learning, King.

OEDIPUS

I know. Don't think that I've been idle there.
Twice I have sent for him at Creon's bidding.
I cannot understand what keeps him so.

CHORUS

At least we can dismiss those other tall old tales.

OEDIPUS

What tales? I must hear them all.

CHORUS

How he met his death through traveling vagabonds.

OEDIPUS

I've heard that too. We have no witnesses, however.

CHORUS

And he'd be a brazen man indeed who could rest in
                                                  peace
  after all your menaces.

OEDIPUS

Mere words will not stay one whom murder never could.

CHORUS

And yet there's one to meet the challenge. Look:
They're leading in the holy prophet,
  sole temple of incarnate truth on earth.

[*The old blind prophet* TIRESIAS *is led in by a boy*]

OEDIPUS

Come, great mystic, Tiresias—intuitive,
  didactic master of the finite and the infinite—

Though you cannot see it you must surely feel
  the overwhelming weight of all this city's woes.
You are our last refuge, Pontiff, and our help.

Apollo, if you have not heard the news,
  has sent back to us who sent to him,
  an answer saying: "No deliverance from the plague
  except you seek and find the Laius killers
  and punish such with death or banishment."
Now, sir, do not begrudge the smallest hint
  your skill from birds or any other omen can elicit.
Save yourself, the city, and save me.
Save us from this whole corruption of the dead.
We are in your hands.
What more rewarding for a man
  than stir himself to help where help he can?

[*There is an ominous pause before* TIRESIAS *answers*]

TIRESIAS

Oh, what anguish to be wise where wisdom is a loss!
I thought I knew this well. What made me come?

OEDIPUS

What makes you come so full of gloom?

TIRESIAS

Please send me home.
Take up your load and I'll take mine.
Believe me, it is better so.

OEDIPUS

What? Refuse to speak?
Is that fair and loyal to your city?

TIRESIAS

Ah, fair speech! If yours were only so
  I should not shy away.

OEDIPUS

By all the gods, do not deny us what you know.
We ask you, all of us, on bended knees.

TIRESIAS

All ignorant! And I refuse to link my utterance
   with a downfall such as yours.

OEDIPUS

You mean, you know and will not say?
You'd rather sacrifice us all and let the city rot?

TIRESIAS

I'd rather keep you and me from harm.
Don't press me uselessly. My lips are sealed.

OEDIPUS

What, nothing? You miserable old man!
You'd drive a stone to fury. Do you still refuse?
Your flinty heart set in hopeless stubbornness?

TRESIAS

My flinty heart! Oh, if you could only see
   what lurks in yours you would not chide me so.

OEDIPUS

Hear that? What man alive, I ask,
   could stand such insults to our sovereignty and state?

TIRESIAS

It will out in time. What if I hold my tongue?

OEDIPUS

Out in time! Then why not say it now?

TIRESIAS

No. I've had my say.
So choose your rage and fume away.

[TIRESIAS *begins to move off*]

OEDIPUS

Indeed I shall. I do. I vent it all on you.
Yes, you, you planned this thing,
    and I suspect you of the very murder even,
    all but the actual stroke.
And if you had your eyes
    I'd say you played that chief part too.

[TIRESIAS *turns back*]

TIRESIAS

Would you so? Then I shall charge you to abide
    by the very curse you trumpeted just now.
From this day forth keep far
    from every person here and me:
The rotting canker in the State is you.

OEDIPUS

Insolence!
And dare you think you're safe?

TIRESIAS

Yes safe. For truth has made me strong.

OEDIPUS

What truth? Hardly learned from your profession!

TIRESIAS

No. Learned from you; who force it out of me.

OEDIPUS

Force what? Say it again. I must have it straight.

TIRESIAS

Was it not straight? You'd bait and goad me on?

OEDIPUS

It made no sense. So speak it out again.

TIRESIAS

I say, the murderer of the man
  whose murder you pursue is you.

OEDIPUS

What! A second time? This you will regret.

TIRESIAS

Shall I add to it and make you angrier still?

OEDIPUS

To your heart's content. Mouth away!

TIRESIAS

I say that you and your most dearly loved
Are wrapped together in a hideous sin, blind to the hor-
                                         ror of it.

OEDIPUS

You think you can go on blabbering unscathed?

TIRESIAS

Unscathed indeed, if truth is strength.

OEDIPUS

It is. But not for you, you purblind man:
  in ears and mind and vision.

TIRESIAS

Poor fool! These very gibes you mouth at me
  will soon be hurled by every mouth at you.

OEDIPUS

You can't hurt me, you night-hatched thing!
Me or any man who lives in light.

TIRESIAS

You're right. I'm not the one that fate casts for your fall.
Apollo is enough. It's in his able hands.

OEDIPUS

[*remembering that it was* CREON *who urged him to send
for* TIRESIAS, *Apollo's priest*]

Creon? Of course! Was it you or he that thought up
                                                  that?

TIRESIAS

Hardly Creon. You are your own worst enemy.

OEDIPUS

Oh wealth and sovereignty! Statecraft surpassing art!
Oh life so pinnacled on fame!
What ambushed envy dogs your trail!
And for a kingship which the State put in my hands,
  all given, never asked.

So this is what he wants, Creon the loyal,
  Creon so long my friend!
Stealing up to overthrow and snatch!

Suborning sorcerers, like this vamper-up of plots,
   this hawking conjurer, a genius born blind
   with eyes for gain. Yes you. Tell me,
   when did you ever play the prophet straight?
Or why when the bitch-dog Sphinx of riddles sang,
   you never spoke a thing to break the spell?
And yet her riddle called for insight trained—
   no traveler's guess—
   which you plainly showed you did not have
   either from theology or birds.
But I, the Oedipus who stumbled here without a hint,
   could snuff her out by human wit,
   not taking cues from birds.
And I'm the one you want to topple down
   to give yourself a place by Creon's throne.
Oh! Do not be surprised if this plot of yours
   to brand me as a scapegoat
   turns around and brands you and him.
And were you not as doting as you seem,
   I'd lash you with the lessons of your fraud.

[CHORUS *leader steps forward, holding up a hand in restraint*]

CHORUS

Forgive us, Oedipus, but this is anger.
He spoke in anger too. And both beside the point.
What we want to know
   is how best to carry out the god's designs.

TIRESIAS

Perhaps you are a king, but I reign too—
   in words. I'll have my equal say.
I'm not your servant. No, I serve Apollo.
So don't ever mark me down as Creon's myrmidon.
I'm blind, you say; you mock at that!
I say you see and still are blind—appallingly:
Blind to your origins and to a union in your house.
Yes, ask yourself where you are from?

You'd never guess what hate is dormant in your home
  or buried with your dear ones dead,
  or how a mother's and a father's curse
Will one day scourge you with its double thongs
  and whip you staggering from the land.
It shall be night where now you boast the day.

Then where shall your yelp of horror not resound,
Where round the world not ring,
  echoing from Mount Cithaeron,
  when at last you see—yes soon—
What portless port this palace and this marriage was you
                              made,
  scudding in before a lucky breeze?
What flood of sorrows—ah! you do not dream—
  will pull you down and level off your pride
To make it match your children
  and the creature that you are.
Go on then, hurl abuse
  at everything that I or Creon say.
No man alive shall see his life so ground away.

OEDIPUS

[*stepping forward threateningly*]

Dear gods! Must I listen to this thing?
Look it dawdles! Wants to wallow in perdition!
Does not turn in panic from my home!

TIRESIAS

You called me here. I never would have come.

OEDIPUS

Nor I have ever summoned you
  if I'd known you'd go foaming at the mouth.

TIRESIAS

A born fool of course to you am I,
  and yet to parents you were born from, wise.

OEDIPUS

Parents? Wait! Who was I born from after all?

TIRESIAS

[*stoppping and turning*]

This very day will furnish you a birthday and a death.

OEDIPUS

What a knack you have for spouting riddles!

TIRESIAS

And you, of course, for solving them!

OEDIPUS

Go on! You challenge there my strongest point.

TIRESIAS

Oh yes! Your lucky strain. Your royal road to ruin.

OEDIPUS

A ruin that saved the State. That's good enough for me.

TIRESIAS

[*turning his back*]

I'll take my leave, then.
Your hand, boy—home.

OEDIPUS

Yes, take him home. Good riddance too!
You're nothing but a nuisance here,
  and one I can do without.

TIRESIAS

[*turning face-about*]

You'll not be rid of me
  until I've spoken what I came to say.
You do not frighten me. There's not a thing
  that you can do to hurt.
I tell you this:
  the man you've searched for all along
  with threats and fanfares
  for the murder of King Laius,
That man, I say, is here:
  a stranger in our midst, they thought,
  but in a moment you shall *see*
  him openly displayed a Theban born,
  and shattered by the honor. Blind
  instead of seeing, beggar
  instead of rich,
He'll grope his way in foreign parts, tapping out his way
  with stick in hand.
Oh yes, detected in his very heart of home:
  his children's father and their brother,
  son and husband to his mother,
  bed-rival to his father and assassin.
Ponder this and go inside,
And when you think you've caught me at a lie,
  then come and tell me I'm not fit to prophesy.

[TIRESIAS *lets his boy lead him away.* OEDIPUS *waits, then
stomps into the palace*]

SECOND CHORAL ODE

[*The Elders, spurred on by the proclamation of* OEDIPUS, *begin to imagine with righteous and indignant anticipation what shall be the fate of the man whose sin has plunged Thebes in misery. The meter is swift and resolute. Then they remember the baffling threat of* TIRESIAS *and they catch their breath at the unthinkable possibility that Oedipus himself may be implicated (Strophe and Antistrophe II).*]

Strophe I

Show me the man the speaking stone from Delphi damned
Whose hands incarnadine
Achieved the master stroke of master murdering.
Faster than horses that beat on the wind he must fly.
The son of Zeus caparisoned in light and fire
Is on his heels.
The pack of sure-foot Fates will track him down.

Antistrophe I

A Voice that coruscates from high Parnassian snows
Leaps down like light.
Apollo to the hunt will run the man to earth
Through savage woods and stony caverns.
A lone wounded bull he limps, lost and alone,
Dodging living echoes
From the mantic earth that sting and gad around him.

Strophe II

Terrible auguries tear me and trouble me:
The seer's divining.
I cannot assent. I cannot deny.
Deserted by words,
I live on hopes—all blind for today and blind for
                                        tomorrow.
A division between the House of Laius and Oedipus
Yesterday or today

I knew not, nor know of a quarrel
Or a reason or challenge to challenge
The fame of Oedipus,
Though I seek to avenge the curious death
Of the Labdacid king.

Antistrophe II

Zeus and Apollo are wise and discern
The conditions of man.
But oh among men where is there proof
That a prophet can know
More than me, a man? Yet wisdom can surpass
Wisdom in a man. But nevertheless I'll not
Be quick to judge
Before the proof. For once
The winged and female Sphinx
Challenged him and found him sound
And a friend of the city. So never in my mind at least
Shall he be guilty of crime.

SECOND EPISODE

[CREON *enters, distraught*]

CREON

Good citizens, I hurry here
   shocked into your presence by a monstrous charge
   laid on me by Oedipus the King.
If he thinks in all this turmoil of our times
   that any word or act of mine
   was ever done in malice, done to harm,
I'd rather end my life than live so wronged.
For this is not a trifling calumny
   but full catastrophe:
   to find myself called traitor;
   traitor to my town,
   to you, and to my friends.

CHORUS

We are convinced the taunt was made in anger,
  not coolly uttered by a mind at calm.

CREON

It was uttered, then? Said that I
  had got the seer to tell a tale of lies?

CHORUS

It was said. We cannot fathom why.

CREON

But said with steady eyes, steady mind—
  this onslaught made against my name?

CHORUS

I do not know.
I turn my eyes away from what my sovereign does.
But look! He's coming from the house himself.

[OEDIPUS *comes raging in*]

OEDIPUS

What? You again? You dare come back?
Have the face to put your foot inside my door?
You the murderer so self-proved,
  the self-condemned filcher of my throne?
In heaven's name, what cowardice or lunacy
  did you detect in me
  to give you gall to do it?
Did you think that I
  would never spot such treachery,
  such slinking jobbery,
  or that when I did I'd not be one to fight?
What madman's game is this:
To go out hunting crowns
  unbacked by friends and money,

when crowns are only won
by many friends and well-crammed money-bags?

CREON

Wait! Listen to my answer to your charge.
And when you've heard me, judge.

OEDIPUS

No. You're too good at talking. And I'm not good at
hearing
one found so laden with malevolence.

CREON

We'll deal first with that very point.

OEDIPUS

That very point, we'll leave alone:
that you're no traitor, eh?

CREON

If you really think a stubborn mind is something to be
proud of,
you're not thinking straight.

OEDIPUS

And if you really think a brother-in-law
can get away with murder, you're not thinking at all.

CREON

All right, then—tell me what I've done.
What's the crime I've wronged you with?

OEDIPUS

Did you or did you not urge me to send
for that reverend frothy-mouthing seer?

CREON

I did. And I still stand by that advice.

OEDIPUS

Then how long is it since Laius . . .

CREON

Laius? I don't follow the connection.

OEDIPUS

Disappeared—died—was mysteriously dispatched?

CREON

Old calendars long past would tell us that.

OEDIPUS

And was this—this "prophet" in his practice then?

CREON

He was, and just as wise, just as honored.

OEDIPUS

And did he at any time then speak of me?

CREON

No. At least never in my hearing.

OEDIPUS

And you did nothing to investigate his death?

CREON

Of course we did: a full commission, and nothing learnt.

OEDIPUS

But the all-seeing seer did not step forward and all see?

CREON

That I cannot answer for and shall not venture an
                                              opinion.

OEDIPUS

You could answer very well—at least upon a certain
                                              point.

CREON

What point is that? If I know, I won't hold it back.

OEDIPUS

Just this: were you not hand-in-glove with him,
  he never would have thought of pinning Laius's death
                                              on me.

CREON

What prompted him, only you can tell.
  Now *I* should like to ask, and you can do the answering.

OEDIPUS

Ask away, but don't expect to find a murderer.

CREON

Well then, are you married to my sister?

OEDIPUS

I am. Why should I deny it?

CREON

And reign equally with her over all the realm?

OEDIPUS

I do, and do my best to grant her every wish.

CREON

And of this twosome do I make an equal third?

OEDIPUS

Exactly! Which is why you make so false a friend.

CREON

No. Try to reason it as I must reason it.
Who would choose uneasy dreams to don a crown
   when all the kingly sway
   can be enjoyed without?
I could not covet kingship for itself
   when I can be a king by other means.
All my ambitions now
   are satisfied through you, without anxiety,
But once a king, all hedged in by constraint.
How could I suit myself with power and sovereignty as
                           now,
If power and sovereignty once grasped were grasped in
                           pain?
I am not so simple as to seize the symbol
   when I can have the sweet reality:
Now smiled upon by all, saluted now,
   now drawn aside by suitors to the King,
   my ear their door to hope.
Why should I let this go, this ease, and reach for cares?
A mind at peace does not engender wars.
Treason never was my bent, nor I
   a man who parleys with an anarchist.

Test me. Go to Delphi. Ask
   if I have brought back lies for prophecies.
And do not stop,
   but if you find me plotting with a fortuneteller,

take me, kill me, full-indicted
on a double not a single count:
not yours alone but mine.
Oh, do not judge me on a mere report, unheard!
No justice brands the good and justifies the bad.
Drive friendship out, I say, and you drive out
life itself, one's sweetest bond.
Time will teach you well. The honest man needs time,
The sinner but a single day to bare his crime.

CHORUS

He speaks well, sire. The circumspect should care.
Swift thinking never makes sure thought.

OEDIPUS

Swift thinking must step in to parry
where swift treachery steps in to plot.
Must I keep mum until his perfect plans
are more than match for mine?

CREON

Then what is it you want—my banishment?

OEDIPUS

Banishment? Great heavens, no! I want you dead:
A lesson to all of how much envy's worth.

CREON

So adamant! So full of disbelief!

OEDIPUS

Only a fool would believe in a rabid man.

CREON

Rabid? It's clear you're not thinking straight.

OEDIPUS

Straight enough for me.

CREON

Then why not for me as well?

OEDIPUS

What! For a treason-monger?

CREON

You make no sense.

OEDIPUS

I make decisions.

CREON

Crazed decisions!

OEDIPUS

Hear him Thebes! My own poor Thebes!

CREON

Not just yours. My city too.

CHORUS

Princes, please!
Look. Jocasta hurries from the house:
   a timely balm on both your hurts.
You must compose your quarrel.

[JOCASTA *hurries in*]

JOCASTA

You wretched men! Out on all this senseless clatter!
Shame to wrangle over private wrongs,

with Thebes our city in her agonies!
Get back home, sir, you, and Creon you
　　into your house.
Stop turning trifles into tragedies.

CREON

Trifles, sister! Oedipus your husband
　　plans to do me devilish harm, with choice of dooms:
　　exile from my father's land or death.

OEDIPUS

Exactly that, my wife, I've caught him in a plot,
　　against my very person.
　　So cleverly devised.

CREON

May I be stricken dead if I be guilty
　　in the smallest part of what you charge!

JOCASTA

For the gods' sakes, listen, Oedipus.
　　He's sworn by all the gods, in front of us,
　　for me and for us all.

CHORAL DIALOGUE

Strophe I

CHORUS

Believe her, King, believe. Be willing to be wise.

OEDIPUS

What! You'd have me yield?

CHORUS

He's never told you lies
before. He's sworn. Be kind.

OEDIPUS

You know for what you plead?

CHORUS

We know.

OEDIPUS

Explain.

CHORUS

Do not impeach a friend or lead
him to disgrace; his oath annulled upon a word.

OEDIPUS

It's come to that? My banishment or death preferred
to what you want for him?

Strophe II

CHORUS

No, by Helios, no, god of the primal sun!
Call gladless death upon me—godless, friendless—
If that be in my mind.
The dying land undoes me,
Sorrow heaped on sadness
Now to see you and him—combine in madness.

OEDIPUS

Go then, let him go, though I go
abundantly to die,
or flung from here and fated;

Yours not his the cry that breaks me.
He a thing that's hated.

CREON

Yes, how you hate, even in your yielding!
But passion spent, compunction follows.
Such men justly bear the tempers they created.

OEDIPUS

Get yourself gone then! Out of my sight!

[CREON *leaves, while* OEDIPUS *continues to stand there disappointed and shaken*]

Antistrophe I

CHORUS

Madam, why delay to lead him away?

JOCASTA

I stay . . . to know.

CHORUS

Hot and hasty words, suspicion and dismay . . .

JOCASTA

From both?

CHORUS

From both.

JOCASTA

What words?

CHORUS

Enough! Enough! The agony! O let it alone!
Let it sleep with all its pain.

OEDIPUS

Very well, but understand
You've numbed me to the heart by your demand.

Antistrophe II

CHORUS

Sire, I've said it more than once
How insensate we'd be, what crass
And total fools to abdicate
From you who set this foundering ship,
This suffering realm, back on her course
And now again can take the helm.

[End of Choral Dialogue. JOCASTA *gently leads* OEDIPUS
aside]

JOCASTA

In the name of all the gods, my king, inform me too
   what in the world has worked you to this rage?

OEDIPUS

Willingly, my wife—so more to me than these.
It's Creon; he has played me false.

JOCASTA

What's the charge? Tell me clearly—what's the quarrel?

OEDIPUS

He makes me murderer of Laius.

JOCASTA

His own invention or on evidence?

OEDIPUS

Ah! The fox: he sends along a mouthing seer
　　and keeps his own lips lily pure.

JOCASTA

Oh then, altogether leave behind
　　these cares and be persuaded and consoled.
There is no art of seership known to man.
I have my proof. Yes, short and certain proof.
Once long ago there came to Laius
　　from—let's not suppose Apollo personally
　　but from his ministers—an oracle,
Which said that fate would make him meet his end
　　through a son, a son of his and mine.
Well, there was a murder, yes,
　　but done by brigands in another land, they say,
Where three highways meet,
　　and secondly, the son, not three days old,
Is left by Laius (through other hands of course)
　　upon a trackless hillside,
　　his ankles riveted together.
So there! Apollo fails to make the son
　　his father's murderer, and the father
　　(Laius sick with dread) murdered by his son.
All foreseen by fate and seers, of course,
　　and all to be forgotten.
If the god insists on tracking down the truth,
　　why then, let the god himself get on the track.

OEDIPUS

My queen, each word that strikes my ear
　　has shattered peace, struck at my very soul.

JOCASTA

You start! What pale memory passes now?

OEDIPUS

Laius was killed—I thought I caught the words—
  where three highways meet?

JOCASTA

So they said. That is how the story goes.

OEDIPUS

The place? Where did the mishap fall?

JOCASTA

A land called Phocis,
  at a spot where the road from Delphi
  meets the road from Daulia.

OEDIPUS

And the time? How many years ago?

JOCASTA

A little before you came to power here
  the news was made public in the town.

OEDIPUS

O Zeus, what plaything will you make of me?

JOCASTA

Why, Oedipus, what nightmare thought has touched you
                    now?

OEDIPUS

Don't ask! Not yet! . . . Laius, tell me, his age? His
                    build?

JOCASTA

Tall, the first soft bloom of silver in his hair;
   in form, not far removed from yours.

OEDIPUS

Oh lost! Yes, surely lost!
   self-damned, I think, just now and self-deceived.

JOCASTA

Self-what, my king?
   that look you give, it chills.

OEDIPUS

I am afraid—afraid the eyeless seer has seen.
But wait: one thing more . . .

JOCASTA

Yes? It frightens me, but ask. I'll try to tell.

OEDIPUS

Did he set out in simple state
   or with an ample bodyguard as king?

JOCASTA

Five men in all, and one a herald.
   A single chariot for the King.

OEDIPUS

It's all too clear . . .
My wife, where did you get these details from?

JOCASTA

A servant. The only man who got away.

OEDIPUS

Is he in the house by chance?

JOCASTA

No, for the moment he was back and saw
   you reigning in dead Laius's place,
   he begged me, pressed my hand,
   to send him to the country, far from Thebes,
   where he could live a shepherd's life.
And so I sent him. Though a slave,
   I thought he'd more than earned this recompense.

OEDIPUS

Could we have him here without delay?

JOCASTA

Certainly. But what should make you ask?

OEDIPUS

There may be things, my wife, that I have said
   best left unsaid, which makes me want him here.

JOCASTA

He shall be here. But tell me, my king,
   may I not also know what it is unnerves you so?

OEDIPUS

You shall,
   for I have passed into territories of fear,
   such threatenings of fate,
   I welcome you, my truest confidante.

My father was Corinthian, Polybus,
My mother Dorian, called Mérope.
I was the city's foremost man until
   a certain incident befell, a curious incident,
   though hardly worth the ferment that it put me in.

At dinner once,
   a drunkard in his cups bawled out,
   "Aha! You're not your father's son."
All that day I fretted, hardly able to contain my hurt.
But on the next, straightway I went to ask
   my mother and my father,
   who were shocked at such a random slur.
I was relieved by their response, and yet
   the thing had hatched a scruple in my mind which grew
   so deep it made me steal away from home
   to Delphi, to the oracle, and there
   Apollo—never hinting what I came to hear—
   packs me home again, my ears ringing
   with some other things he blurted out;
   horrible disgusting things:
How mating with my mother I must spawn
   a progeny to make men shudder,
   having been my father's murderer.

Oh, I fled from there, I measured out
   the stars to put all heaven in between
   the land of Corinth and such a damned destiny.
And as I went, I stumbled on the very spot
   where this king you say has met his end.

I'll . . . I'll tell the truth to you, my wife.
As I reached this triple parting of the ways,
   a herald and a man like you described
   in a colt-drawn chariot came.
The leading groom—the old man urging him—
   tried to force me off the road. The groom
   jostled me and I in fury
   landed him a blow.
Which when the old man sees,
   he waits till I'm abreast,
Then from his chariot cracks down on me,
   full on my head,
   a double-headed club.
He more than paid for it. For in a trice
   this hand of mine had felled him with a stick
   and rolled him from the chariot stunned.

I killed him. I killed them all.
Ah! If Laius is this unknown man,
   there's no one in this world so doomed as I.
There's no one born so god-abhorred:
   a man whom no one, citizen or stranger,
   can let into his house or even greet—
   a man to force from homes.
And who but I have done it all? Myself,
   to fix damnation on myself!
   To clasp a dead man's wife with filthy hands:
   these hands by which he fell.
Not hell-born then? Not rotten to the core?
A wretch who has to flee, yet fled cannot go home
   to see my own,
Or I will make my mother wife, my father dead:
   my father, Polybus, who reared and gave me life.
Forbid, forbid, most holy gods!
Never let that day begin.
I'd rather disappear from man than see
   myself so beggared, dyed so deep in sin.

CHORUS

King, you tell us frightening things, but wait
   until you've heard the witness speak. Have hope.

OEDIPUS

Yes, all my hope upon a herdsman now,
   and I must wait until he comes.

JOCASTA

But when he comes, what is it you want to hear?

OEDIPUS

Just this: if his account is yours, I'm clear.

JOCASTA

But what was my account? What did I say?

OEDIPUS

Why, several bandits in your account,
  he claimed, cut down the King.
If he will keep to *several*, I, as only one,
  am not the killer, not the same.
But if he says it was a lone man journeying—ah then!—
  the verdict tilts too heavily to me.

JOCASTA

Rest assured; his account was that, exactly that,
. He cannot cancel what he said.
The whole town heard, not I alone.
And even if he tries to change a word,
  he still can never make—oh surely, King!—
  the death of Laius tally with the oracle,
  which said it had to happen through a son of mine . . .
  poor babe, who never killed a thing
  but himself was killed—oh long before!
After this, I'll never change my look from left to right
  to suit a prophecy.

OEDIPUS

I like your reasoning. And yet . . . and yet . . .
  that herdsman—have him here. Do not forget.

JOCASTA

Immediately. But let us go indoors.
All my care is you, and all my pleasure yours.

[OEDIPUS *and* JOCASTA *enter the palace*]

THIRD CHORAL ODE

[*The Elders seem at first merely to be expressing a lyrical
admiration for piety and purity of heart, but before the
end of the ode we see that the reputation itself of* OEDIPUS
is at stake. JOCASTA's *blatant impiety has shocked the*
CHORUS *into realizing that if divine prophecies cannot go
unfulfilled and man's insolence unpunished, then* OEDIPUS
*himself, whoever he is, must be weighed in the balance.
It is too late to go back. A choice will have to be made.
They call desperately on Zeus.*]

Strophe I

O purity of deed and sweet intent,
Enshrine me in your grace
A minister to radiant laws
Heaven-born which have
No father but Olympus nor
Fading genesis from man.
Great is God in them
And never old
Whom no oblivion lulls.

Antistrophe I

Pride engenders power, pride,
Banqueting on vanities
Mistaken and mistimed;
Scaling pinnacles to dash
A foot against Fate's stone.
But the true and patriotic man
Heaven never trips to fall.
So I for one shall never desert
The god who is our champion.

Strophe II

But what if a brazen man parade
In word or deed

Impiety and brash disdain
Of principalities and canons?
Then dog him doom and pay him pride
Wages for his haughty greed,
His sacrilege and folly.
What shield is there for such a man
Against all heaven's arrows?
Could I celebrate such wantonness
And celebrate the dance?

Antistrophe II

I shall not worship at the vent
Where oracles from earth are breathed;
Nor at Abae's shrine and not
Olympia, unless these oracles
Are justified, writ large to man.
Zeus, if king of kings you are,
Then let this trespass not go hidden
From you and your great eye undying.
The Laius prophecies are turned to lies;
They fade away with reverence gone
And honor to Apollo.

THIRD EPISODE

[JOCASTA *hurries in from the palace with a garlanded olive branch and a burning censer in her hands*]

JOCASTA

Men of State, I have a new design:
With these garlands and with incense in my hands
   to call at all the shrines.
For rampant fancies in a legion raid
   the mind of Oedipus. He is so far from sense
   he cannot gauge the present from the past
   but pins his soul to every word of fear.

All my advice is bankrupt; I address
   myself to you Apollo, whose Lycean shrine
   is nearest to these rites and prayers:
That you may work some way to make us clean.
For we are gone to pieces at the sight
   of him the steersman of the ship
   astray by fright.

[*While* JOCASTA *is standing in prayer a* MESSENGER *from Corinth enters*]

MESSENGER

Can you tell me please, good sirs,
   where is the palace of King Oedipus,
   or better, where's the King?

CHORUS

This is his palace, sir, and he's within.
This lady is his wife and mother . . . of his children.

MESSENGER

Heaven bless her always and bless hers:
   the perfect wife blessed perfectly with him.

JOCASTA

And you sir, too, be blessed for your remark . . .
But are you here to ask us news or give?

MESSENGER

To give it, madam. Happy news
   both for your house and husband.

JOCASTA

Happy news? From where?

MESSENGER

From Corinth, my lady. Oh a pleasing piece of news!
Or I'd think so . . . Perhaps a little bittersweet.

JOCASTA

What's bittersweet? What's half-and-half to please?

MESSENGER

King Elect of Corinth is he:
So runs the order-in-council there.

JOCASTA

How so? The old man Polybus still reigns.

MESSENGER

No more. For death has sealed him in his grave.

JOCASTA

What? Is Oedipus's father dead?

MESSENGER

Yes, dead. It's true. On my life he's dead.

[JOCASTA *excitedly turns to servant girl*]

JOCASTA

Quick girl—off and tell your master this!
Aha! Forecasts of the gods where are you now?
This is the man that Oedipus was terrified to kill, so fled;
And now, without the slightest push from him, he's dead.

[*Enter* OEDIPUS]

OEDIPUS

Jocasta, dearest wife,
    why have you called me from the palace here?

JOCASTA

Just listen to this man and fill your ears.
How dwindled are the grand predictions of Apollo!

OEDIPUS

Who is this? What has he come to say?

JOCASTA

A man from Corinth, come to let you know
  your father is no more. Old Polybus is dead.

OEDIPUS

What? Let me have it from your mouth, good sir.

MESSENGER

Why, to give you first news first, he's gone.
Be quite assured—he's dead.

OEDIPUS

Through treason or disease?

MESSENGER

A little touch will tip the old to sleep.

OEDIPUS

He died a natural death, then? Poor old man!

MESSENGER

A natural death, by right of many years.

OEDIPUS

Aha, my wife! So we are done
  with delving into Pythian oracles,
  this jangled mongering with birds on high,
  which foretold—yes, had it all arranged—

that I should kill my father. Ha! He's dead
and under sods, while here I stand
my sword still in its scabbard . . .
or did he pine for me? And did I kill him so?
Well, he's dead, and may he rest in peace in Hades realm
with all those prophecies—worth nothing now.

JOCASTA

Worth nothing—as I told you even then.

OEDIPUS

You told me, yes, but I was sick with fear.

JOCASTA

Forget it all. Give none of it a thought.

OEDIPUS

There's still that scruple of my mother's bed.

JOCASTA

How can a man have scruples
   when it's only Chance that's king?
There's nothing certain, nothing preordained.
We should live as carefree as we may.
Forget this silly thought of mother-marrying.
Why, many men in dreams have married mothers,
And he lives happiest who makes the least of it.

OEDIPUS

Everything you say would make good sense
   were my mother not alive—she is;
   so all your comfort cannot quiet me.

JOCASTA

At least your father's death has lightened up the scene.

OEDIPUS

It has, but now I fear a living woman.

MESSENGER

A woman, sir? Who ever could she be?

OEDIPUS

Mérope, old man, who lives with Polybus.

MESSENGER

But what's in her that she can make you fear?

OEDIPUS

A dire warning sent from heaven, my friend.

MESSENGER

Some secret too horrible to tell?

OEDIPUS

No, you may be told.
Apollo once declared that I
   would come to couple with my mother,
   and with these very hands of mine
   spill out the life-blood of my father.
All of which has put me far and long from Corinth,
   in sweet prosperity maybe,
But what's so sweet as looking into parents' eyes?

MESSENGER

Is this the fear that drove you out of Corinth?

OEDIPUS

Exactly that, old man, and not to kill my father.

MESSENGER

Well, my King, since I came to save,
  why don't I loose you from that worry too?

OEDIPUS

Ah! If you could, I'd heap you with rewards.

MESSENGER

Ah! to be frank, that's why I came . . . to bring you
                                 home,
  and do myself some good.

OEDIPUS

No, not home. I'll not go near a parent still.

MESSENGER

My son, it's plain you don't know what you're at.

OEDIPUS

Speak out, old man. In the name of heaven—what?

MESSENGER

Well, you've fled from home because of this?

OEDIPUS

Yes, the fear Apollo may be proven right.

MESSENGER

And you, because of your parents, a criminal?

OEDIPUS

Yes, old man, it's that. I'm haunted by that dread.

MESSENGER

Then, don't you understand, you're terrified for nothing.

OEDIPUS

Nothing? How—when I *am* their son.

MESSENGER

Because Polybus and you were worlds apart.

OEDIPUS

Worlds apart? He was my father, wasn't he?

MESSENGER

No more nor less than I who tell you this.

OEDIPUS

No more nor less than you? Than nothing then.

MESSENGER

Exactly so. He never gave you life, no more than I.

OEDIPUS

Then, whatever made him call me son?

MESSENGER

You were a gift. He took you from my arms.

OEDIPUS

A gift? But he loved me as his own.

MESSENGER

He had no children of his own to love.

OEDIPUS

And this gift of me you gave—was I freeborn or bought?

MESSENGER

Discovered . . . in a woody mountain dell of Cithaeron.
[JOCASTA *moves away. She has gone pale*]

OEDIPUS

On Theban hills? What made you wander there?

MESSENGER

On those hills I used to graze my flock.

OEDIPUS

What! A shepherd out for hire?

MESSENGER

And on that day your savior too, my son.

OEDIPUS

My savior? Was I in pain when you took me in your
                                                    arms?

MESSENGER

The ankles of your feet could tell you that.

OEDIPUS

Ah, don't remind me of that ancient hurt.

MESSENGER

I loosed the pin that riveted your feet.

OEDIPUS

My birthmark and my brand from babyhood!

MESSENGER

Which gave you also your unlucky name.*

OEDIPUS

Was this my mother's doing or my father's?
For the gods' sakes say!

[JOCASTA *hides her face in her hands*]

MESSENGER

That, I do not know. The man who gave you me could
tell.

OEDIPUS

What, received at secondhand? Not found by you?

MESSENGER

Not found by me, but handed over by another shepherd.

OEDIPUS

What shepherd? Could you point him out?

MESSENGER

I think he was known as one of Laius's men.

OEDIPUS

You mean the king who reigned here long ago?

*"Swollen-foot."

MESSENGER

The same. He was a herdsman of that king.

OEDIPUS

Could I see him? Is he still alive?

MESSENGER

Your own people could tell you best.

[OEDIPUS *turns to the* CHORUS]

OEDIPUS

Does any man here present know this herdsman he is
                                        talking of:
    either seen him in the fields or hereabouts?
The time has come for full discovery.

CHORUS

I think he means that herdsman, sir,
    you asked to see before.
Jocasta here is surest judge of that.

[*They all turn toward* JOCASTA, *who stands transfixed*]

OEDIPUS

Come, madam, do you know the man we sent for once
                                        before?
Is he the man he means?

JOCASTA

[*wildly*]

Which man? What matters who he means? Why ask?
Forget it all. It's not worth knowing.

OEDIPUS

Forget it all? I can't stop now.
Not with all my birth clues in my hands.

JOCASTA

In the name of heaven, don't proceed!
For your own life's sake, stop!
And I've been tortured long enough.

OEDIPUS

Oh come! It won't be you that is disgraced
    even if I'm proved a thrice-descended slave.

[JOCASTA *throws herself before him and clutches his knees*]

JOCASTA

Yet be persuaded, please. Do *not* proceed.

OEDIPUS

Persuaded from the truth? Pursuing it? I must.

JOCASTA

Though I'm pleading for what's best for you.

OEDIPUS

What's best for me? I'm tired of hearing that.

JOCASTA

[*rising slowly*]

God help you, Oedipus! Hide it from you who you are.

OEDIPUS

Will someone go and fetch the herdsman here?
We'll leave the lady to her high descent.

JOCASTA

Good-bye, my poor deluded, lost and damned!
There's nothing else that I can call you now.

[JOCASTA *rushes into the palace*]

CHORUS

Oedipus, what made the Queen so wildly leave,
   struck dumb? A stillness just before the storm!

OEDIPUS

Storm, then, let it burst!
Born from nothing though I be proved,
   let me find that nothing out.
And let my wife with all a woman's pride
   bridle at my paltry origin.
I do not blush to own I'm Fortune's pampered child.
She will not let me down. She is my mother.
The moons my monthly cousins watched me wax and
                           wane.

My fealty to that family makes me move
   true to myself. My family I shall prove.

FOURTH CHORAL ODE

[*The Elders, forgetting for the moment* JOCASTA's *ominous withdrawal, anticipate the joy of discovering who* OEDIPUS *really is. Ironically, they imagine themselves already celebrating his remarkable origins.*]

Strophe

If I am a prophet with sapient eyes,
Cithaeron you, my mystical mountain,
Tomorrow before the moon's full rise,
Shall shout out your name as the nurse and the mother,
The father as well of our Oedipus.
Then shall we weave our dances around you;
You who have showered our princes with graces.
Ayay, great Apollo! May't please you, ayay!

Antistrophe

Who was your mother, son? Which of the dryads
Did Pan of the mountains have? Was he your father?
Or was it Apollo who haunts the savannas?
Or perhaps Hermes on the heights of Cyllene?
Or was Dionysus god of the pinnacles
Of Helicon's hilltops where he abides
Presented with you by some Helliconian
Nymph, among whom he frequently frolics?

FOURTH EPISODE

[*A figure, old and roughly clad, is seen approaching*]

OEDIPUS

Look, Elders,
   if I may play the prophet too,
   I'd say—although I've never met the man—
   there's the herdsman we've been searching for.
He's old enough and matches this old man.
But you no doubt can better judge than I:
   you've seen the man before.

CHORUS

We know him well.
Laius never had a better servant.

[*The* SHEPHERD *enters, ill at ease.* OEDIPUS *surveys him and turns to the* MESSENGER]

OEDIPUS

First question then to you, Corinthian:
　is he the man you mean?

MESSENGER

The very man.

OEDIPUS

Come here, sir, and look me in the eyes.
Tell me straight: were you ever Laius's?

SHEPHERD

Yes sir, born and bred, sir—never bought.

OEDIPUS

And what was your job? How were you employed?

SHEPHERD

Chiefly as a shepherd, sir.

OEDIPUS

A shepherd where? What was your terrain?

SHEPHERD

[*hedging*]

Sometimes . . . the slopes of Cithaeron
　and sometimes . . . thereabouts.

OEDIPUS

Good, then you've run across this man before?

[*The* SHEPHERD *desperately tries to avoid looking at the* MESSENGER]

SHEPHERD

How'd he be there, sir? . . . What man do you mean,
sir?

OEDIPUS

The man in front of you. Did you ever meet him?

SHEPHERD

Not to remember, sir . . . I couldn't rightly say.

MESSENGER

And no wonder, sire! But let me jog his memory.
I'm sure he won't forget the slopes of Cithaeron
   where for three half-years we were neighbors,
   he and I; he with two herds, I with one:
   six long months, from spring to early autumn.
And when at last the winter came,
   we both drove off our flocks,
   I to my sheepcotes, he back to Laius's folds . . .
Am I right or am I wrong?

SHEPHERD

[*sullenly*]

Aye, you're right. But it was long ago.

MESSENGER

Now tell me this. Do you recall a certain baby boy
   you gave me once to bring up as my own?

SHEPHERD

What're you getting at? What're these questions for?

MESSENGER

Take a look, my friend. He's standing there, your baby
boy.

SHEPHERD

Damn you man! Can you not hold your tongue?

OEDIPUS

Watch your words, old man!
It's you who ought to be rebuked, not he.

SHEPHERD

Great master, please! What have I done wrong?

OEDIPUS

Not answered this man's questions on the baby boy.

SHEPHERD

But, sir, he's rambling nonsense. He doesn't know a thing.

OEDIPUS

You won't talk for pleasure?
Then perhaps you'll talk for pain.

[OEDIPUS *raises a threatening hand*]

SHEPHERD

By all the gods, sir, don't hurt a poor old man.

OEDIPUS

Here, someone twist the wretch's hands behind his back.

[*A palace guard steps forward*]

SHEPHERD

God help me, sir! What is it you must know?

OEDIPUS

The baby he's been speaking of—did you give it him or
not?

SHEPHERD

I did . . . I did . . . I wish I'd died that day.

OEDIPUS

You'll die today, unless you speak the truth.

SHEPHERD

Much sooner, sir, if I speak the truth.

OEDIPUS

This man, it's clear, is playing for time.

SHEPHERD

No, not me, sir! I've already said I gave it him.

OEDIPUS

Then where's it from? Your home or someone else's.

SHEPHERD

Oh not mine, sir! I got it from another.

OEDIPUS

Someone here in Thebes? Of what house?

SHEPHERD

By all the gods, sir, don't ask me any more!

OEDIPUS

If I have to ask again—you're dead.

SHEPHERD

Then . . . from Laius's house . . . that's where it's from.

OEDIPUS

What, a slave? Or someone of his line?

SHEPHERD

Oh sir! Must I bring myself to say it?

OEDIPUS

And I to hear it. Yes, it must be said.

SHEPHERD

They say it was . . . actually his own.
But the Queen inside could probably explain.

OEDIPUS

She, *she* gave it you?

SHEPHERD

Just that, my lord.

OEDIPUS

With what intention?

SHEPHERD

To do away with it.

OEDIPUS

The child's own mother?

SHEPHERD

To escape a prophecy too horrible.

OEDIPUS

What kind of prophecy?

SHEPHERD

A warning that he'd kill his father.

OEDIPUS

In heaven's name, what made you pass him on
  to this old man?

SHEPHERD

Only pity, sir.
I thought he'd take him home and far away.
Never this—oh, never kept for infamy!
For if you are the one he says you are,
Make no mistake: you are a doom-born man.

[OEDIPUS *stares in front of him, then staggers forward*]

OEDIPUS

Lost! Ah lost! At last it's blazing clear.
Light of my days, go dark. I want to gaze no more.
My birth all sprung revealed from those it never should,
Myself entwined with those I never could.
And I the killer of those I never would.

[OEDIPUS *rushes into the palace*]

FIFTH CHORAL ODE

[The Elders, seeing that the cause of OEDIPUS *is lost, break into a desperate lament for the insecurity of all human fame, so bitterly exemplified now in the fall of the once-confident King.]*

Strophe I

Oh the generations of man!
His life is vanity and nothingness.
Is there one, one
Who more than tastes of, thinks of, happiness,
Which in the thinking vanishes?
Yours the text, yours the spell,
I see it in you Oedipus:
Man's pattern of unblessedness.

Antistrophe I

You who aimed so high!
Who hit life's topmost prize—success!
Who—Zeus, oh, who—
Struck and toppled down the griffin-taloned
Deathknell witch, and like a saving tower
Soared above the rotting shambles here:
A sovereign won, supremely blest,
A king of mighty Thebes.

Strophe II

Caught in the end by Time
Who always sees, where Justice sits as judge,
Your unwed wedding's done,
Begetter and begot—O son of Laius!—
Out of sight what sight might not have seen!
My sorrow heaves, my lips lament,
Which drew their breath from you and now
Must quiver and be still.

EPILOGUE

[*A* PALACE OFFICIAL *hurries out from the palace*]

OFFICIAL

Listen, lords most honorable of Thebes:
    forget the House of Labdacus, all filial sympathy,
    if you would stop your ears, hide your eyes,
    not break your hearts against appalling pain.
No rivers—even Ister, even Phasis—
    could flush away, I think, the horrors
    hidden in these walls, where now
    other evils, courted evils self-incurred,
Will bring to light the perfect agony of self-inflicted pain.

CHORUS

Stop. What we've seen already is unbearable.
What further agony will you load on us?

OFFICIAL

I'll tell it quickly and you can quickly hear:
    Jocasta's gone, the Queen.

CHORUS

Dead? Poor lady! How?

OFFICIAL

She killed herself.
You cannot apprehend, you who were not there,
    how horrible it was.
But I was there and what I tell you now
    is stamped upon my memory:
Oh, the struggles of that lost princess!

The moment she had burst into the palace,
    running through the doors demented,
    she made for the bridal bed,

plunging her fingers through her hair
and slamming shut the door behind her.
We heard her sobbing out Laius's name (so long dead),
   recalling the night his love had bred his murderer
And left a mother making cursed children with her son.
"Unhappy bed!" she wailed. "Twice wicked soil!
The father's seedbed nurtured for the mother's son!"

And then she killed herself. How, I do not know.
The final act escaped our eyes—
   all fastened now upon the raving Oedipus,
   who broke upon us, stamping up and down
   and shouting out: "A weapon, quick!
   Where is the brideless bride?
Find me that double breeding ground
   where sown the mother, now has sown the son."
Some instinct of a demigod discovered her to him,
   not us near by. As if led on,
He smashes hollering through the double doors,
   breaking all its bolts, and lunges in.
And there we saw her hanging, twisted, tangled,
   from a halter.
A sight that rings from him a maddened cry.
He frees the noose and lays the wretched woman down,
   then—Oh hideous sequel!—rips from off her dress
   the golden brooches she was wearing,
Holds them up and rams the pins right through his eyes.
"Wicked, wicked eyes!" he gasps,
   "You shall not see me nor my crime,
   not see my present shame.
Go dark for all time blind
   to what you never should have seen, and blind
   to the love this heart has cried to see."

And as this dirge went up, so did his hands
   to strike his founts of sight
   not once but many times.
And all the while his eyeballs gushed
   in bloody dew upon his beard . . .
   no, not dew, no oozing drops—a spurt
   of black-ensanguined rain like hail beat down.

A coupled punishment upon a coupled sin:
   husband and wife one flesh in their disaster—
Their happiness of long ago, true happiness,
   now turned to tears this day,
   to ruin, death, and shame;
No evil absent by whatever cursed name.

CHORUS

Poor man! What agony!

OFFICIAL

He shouts for all the barriers to be unbarred and he
   displayed to all of Thebes, his father's murderer,
   his mother's . . . no, a word too foul to say . . .
   begging to be cast adrift, not rot at home
   as curser and the cursed.
His strength is gone. He needs a helping hand,
   his wound and weakness more than he can bear.
But you will see. The gates are opening. Look:
   a sight that turns all loathing into tears.

[OEDIPUS, *blinded, enters and staggers down the palace
steps*]

CHORAL DIALOGUE

CHORUS

Oh, most inhuman vision!
A world of pain outsuffered and outdone.
What possession in full flush
   has swamped your brain?
What giant of evil beyond all human brawn
   pounced on you with devil's doom?
Oh, the pity and the horror!
I cannot look—and yet so much to ask,
   so much to know, so much to understand.
I cannot look for shuddering.

OEDIPUS

I am deserted, dark,
And where is sorrow stumbling?
Whence flits that voice so near?
Where, demon, will you drive me?

CHORUS

To a doom no voice can speak, no eye regard.

Strophe I

OEDIPUS

Aah! a nightmare mist has fallen
Adamantine black on me—
Abomination closing.
Cry, cry, oh cry again!
Those needle pains:
The pointed echoes of my sinning.

CHORUS

Such great sufferings are not strange
Where a double sorrow requires a double pang.

Antistrophe I

OEDIPUS

Oh you my friends!
Still friends and by my side!
Still staying by the blindman!
Your form eludes, your voice is near;
That voice lights up my darkness.

CHORUS

Man of havoc, how
Could you hate your sight so?
What demon so possessed you?

Strophe II

OEDIPUS

Friends, it was Apollo, spirit of Apollo.
He made this evil fructify.
Oh yes, I pierced my eyes, my useless eyes, why not?
When all that's sweet had parted from my vision.

CHORUS

And so it has; is as you say.

OEDIPUS

Nothing left to see, to love,
No welcome in communion.
Friends, who are my friends,
Hurry me from here,
Hurry off the monster:
That deepest damned and god-detested man.

CHORUS

A man, alas, whose anguish fits his fate.
We could wish that we had never known you.

Antistrophe II

OEDIPUS

Yes, rot that man's unlocking my feet from biting fetters.
Unloosing me from murder to lock me in a blood-love.
Had I only died then, I should not now be leaving
All I love and mine so sadly shattered.

CHORUS

Your wish is also ours.

OEDIPUS

Then I should be free,
Yes, free from parricide:
Not pointed out as wedded
To the one who weaned me.
Now I am god-abandoned,
A son of sin and sorrows
All incest-sealed
With the womb that bore me.
Oh Oedipus, your portion!

CHORUS

But how can we say that your design was good?
To live in blindness? Better live no longer.

[*End of strophic pattern*]

OEDIPUS

Enough of this! Enough of your advice!
It was a good design. Don't tell me otherwise.
My best design!
What kind of eyes should I need
    to gaze upon my father's face in Hades
    or my unhappy mother's:
Those twin victims ruined by me
    for whom I should be hanged?
Or eyes that could be eyes to stare
    into my children's faces?
Joy? No no, a sight of pain
    engendered from those loins.
Or even eyes to view again citadel and tower
    and holy idoled shrine I cast away?
Most cursed I, the prince of princes here in Thebes
    and now pariah self-damned and self-arraigned:
The refuse-heap of heaven on display as son of Laius,
    parading and self-dyed in sin.
What? Eyes to lift and gaze at these?
    No no, there's none!
Rather plug my ears and choke that stream of sound,

stuff the senses of my carcass dumb—
glad to stifle voices with my vision,
and sweet to lift the soul away from hurt.

Pity you, Cithaeron, that you gave me harbor,
　took me in and did not kill me straight;
　that you did not hush my birth from man.
Pity you Polybus and Corinth,
　age-old home I called my father's:
What fair skin you housed around what foulness!
A prince of evil all revealed and son of sin.
And you three roads and dell concealed,
　you copse of oak and straitened triple ways!
　I handed you my blood to drink,
　the chalice of my father's.
What memories have you of my manners then,
　or what I did when afterwards I came here?
You batch of weddings! Birthdays breeding
　seedlings from their very seed:
Fathers, sons and brothers flourishing in foulness
　with brides and wives and mothers
　in a monstrous coupling . . .
Unfit to tell what's too unfit to touch!
My load is mine, don't fear;
　no man could bear so much.

CHORUS

Wait! Here Creon comes to hear your pleas
　and deal with your designs.
He takes your place
　as sole custodian of the State.

OEDIPUS

Ah! What words are left for me to him?
What title to sincerity and trust
　when all my past behavior's proved so wrong?

[*Enter* CREON]

CREON

It's not to scoff or scorn for past behavior, Oedipus,
   that I am here . . .

[*Turns to attendants*]

You there, show some reverence for the dignity of man,
   and blush at least before Apollo's royal sun
   which feeds the world with fire,
   to so display unveiled putrescence
   in its very picture of decay—
Assaulting earth, the heaven's rain, the light of day.
Quickly take him home. A family's ears, a family's eyes,
   alone should know a family's miseries.

OEDIPUS

For the gods' own love, you best of men
   who visit me the worst
   with clemency beyond my dreams,
   grant me one request: I ask it
   for your sake not mine.

CREON

What favor could you want of me?

OEDIPUS

Expel me quickly, purge me far from Thebes
   to where no human voice is heard.

CREON

This I would have done at once
   but first must ask the god's design.

OEDIPUS

The god's design is open, all his oracle is clear:
   kill the impious one, the parricide, kill *me*.

CREON

So ran the words, but in these straits
    it's best to ask the god again what should be done.

OEDIPUS

What! Interrogations still for a thing so down?

CREON

Yes, and even you will now believe the god.

OEDIPUS

I do. But add to it this charge, I beg, this prayer:
    her poor remains still in the house,
    bury them—what tomb you wish.
You must not fail your own with proper rites.
But as for me, my father's city here
    must never harbor me alive,
    so let me live among the hills,
    yes, Cithaeron, that very mountain famed as mine;
Which my father and my mother gave me while they
                                                    lived
    to be my tomb.
There I'll be obedient to the death they planned.
For this I know, no sickness and no natural death
    will sever me from life . . . no, not me,
    preserved from death precisely for disaster.
So let my fortune follow where it will.

Now for my children, first of all my sons.
These you need not care for, Creon. They are men
    and they will always find a livelihood.
But my little girls, that stricken pair of orphans
    whose place at table never missed being set with mine,
    who ate with me, drank from my cup—ah! these
    look after for me, guard them both.

[CREON *goes to fetch* OEDIPUS's *two little daughters,*
ANTIGONE *and* ISMENE. *Meanwhile,* OEDIPUS, *thinking
he is still there, continues to plead*]

If I could only touch them with my hands
    and weep my fill, good Creon, one last time!
Just touch them, please, you generous-hearted prince,
    and think them in my arms as when I saw.

[CREON *returns leading* ANTIGONE *and* ISMENE *by the hand*]

Wait! That sobbing? Don't tell me
    it's my two darlings crying!
Has Creon pitied me and sent me all my heart's desire?
Can that be true?

CREON

It is. I ordered it to stir again your old delight.

OEDIPUS

God bless you, Creon, bless your path through life,
    encompass you with surer joys than mine.
But children where, where are you? Hurry
    into these arms . . . these brother's . . . these
    father's arms—that struck out the light
    and made his face this eyeless mask.
For—oh my little ones!—
    he did not see, he had no knowing,
When he became your father—in full view—
    the sower and the seed.

He cannot see you now but still can weep
    and ponder on those bitter days to come
    which cruel consort with the world will prove.
No public holidays, no carnivals,
    from which you will not hurry home in tears.
And then one day a marriage time will come,
    but who will marry you? Who on this earth will face
    the destiny that dogs our line?
Our record's too replete:
    "This father killed his father,
    tilled the womb again from which he sprang,
    to beget you very children from his bed of birth."

Such will be their gibes,
   so who will want to marry you?
There's none, my children, no not one,
   and life for you is all decline
   to doom and empty spinsterhood.

[*He turns to* CREON]

Listen, Son of Menoeceus,
   now their natural parents are no more,
   they have no other father left but you.
You must not see your blood go down in beggary,
   or watch them roaming husbandless.
You must not leave them to a fate like mine.
Open your heart—they're young,
   bereft of everything unless you furnish it.
Come . . . a promise noble prince . . . your hand!

[CREON *gives his hand*]

My darling little ones, if you could only understand,
   I'd tell you, oh, so many things!
Let this suffice, a simple prayer:
Abide in modesty so may you live
   the happy life your father did not have.

CREON

These tears . . . enough! . . . Now go inside.

OEDIPUS

I must, with bitterness.

CREON

All things have their time.

OEDIPUS

You know my terms?

CREON

I'll know them when you tell me.

OEDIPUS

Then send me far away from home.

CREON

You ask what only the gods can give.

OEDIPUS

The gods? They are my enemy.

CREON

They'll answer all the swifter, then.

OEDIPUS

Ah! Do you mean it?

CREON

What I do not mean, I do not say.

OEDIPUS

Then lead me off.

CREON

Come! Let your children go.

OEDIPUS

No, no, never! Don't take them from me.

CREON

Stop this striving to be master of all.
The mastery you had in life has been your fall.

[CREON *signs to the attendants, who disengage* OEDIPUS *from his children and lead him into the palace.* CREON *follows and the doors are closed. The* CHORUS *groups for the exit march*]

ENVOI

CHORUS

Citizens of our ancestral Thebes,
Look on this Oedipus, the mighty and once masterful:
Elucidator of the riddle,
Envied on his pedestal of fame.
You saw him fall. You saw him swept away.
So, being mortal, look on that last day
And count no man blessed in his life until
He's crossed life's bounds unstruck by ruin still.

OEDIPUS
AT COLONUS

in memory of
Martin W. Tanner
"he setteth his mind to finish
his work, and watcheth
to polish it perfectly."

THE CHARACTERS

OEDIPUS, former king of Thebes

ANTIGONE, his daughter

A COUNTRYMAN of Colonus

CHORUS of Elders of Colonus

ISMENE, sister of Antigone and daughter of Oedipus

THESEUS, king of Athens

CREON, brother-in-law of Oedipus and present ruler
    of Thebes

Bodyguard of Creon

POLYNEICES, son of Oedipus

A MESSENGER

Soldiers and Attendants of Theseus

Servant to Ismene

TIME AND SETTING

Some twenty years have passed since OEDIPUS *blinded himself after discovering that he had murdered his father and married his mother. During much of that time he has been wandering from town to town accompanied by his daughter,* ANTIGONE. CREON, *the regent of Thebes, has turned against him, as also have his two sons, who are now contending for the throne.*

OEDIPUS *is about sixty-five but looks much older. Gaunt, white-haired, dressed in rags (with a beggar's wallet) and leaning on* ANTIGONE, *he slowly climbs the rocky path that leads to the edge of a wood, where the statue of a hero on a horse can be discerned among the trees. It is early afternoon in April.*

Oedipus at Colonus

PROLOGUE

OEDIPUS

So where have we come to now, Antigone, my child,
   this blind old man and you—
   what people and what town?
And who today will dole out charity
   to Oedipus the vagabond?
It's little that I ask, and I make do with less.
Patience is what I've learned from pain;
   from pain and time and my own past royalty.

But, do you see any place, dear girl, where I may sit:
   whether in public ground or sacred grove—
There sit me down
   Just until we've found out where we are.
For we are only wanderers
   and must ask advice of citizens
   and do as they direct.

ANTIGONE

[*looking at her father with concern, and then gazing across the plain toward Athens*]

Poor father! Poor wayworn Oedipus! . . .
I can see the walls and turrets of a town,
   a long way off,
And where we stand is clearly consecrated ground
   luxuriant in laurel, olive, vine,
   and deep in the song of nightingales.

[ANTIGONE *peers into the grove*]

So rest yourself upon this boulder here:
  a rough seat, I know.
But you've come too long a way for an old man.

OEDIPUS

A blind one too! So watch him well and help him down.

ANTIGONE

After all this time, I need no lessons there.

[*She leads him to the rock seat inside the grove and settles
him there*]

OEDIPUS

Now tell me: have you the slightest inkling where we
                                                    are?

ANTIGONE

Well, I know it's Athens, but this spot . . . I've no idea.

OEDIPUS

Of course it's Athens. That much we know from every-
                                      one we've passed.

ANTIGONE

Then shall I go and ask what this place is called?

OEDIPUS

Do child, if there's any sign of life.

ANTIGONE

Oh, but there must be!
In fact I don't even have to go. I see a man approaching.

OEDIPUS

What! Coming our way? Coming here?

ANTIGONE

He's almost on us . . . Quick, you speak, Father—
    here he is.

[*Enter a* COUNTRYMAN *of Colonus*]

OEDIPUS

Excuse me, good sir, my daughter here
    whose eyes are mine as they are hers,
    tells me you are passing by,
Just in time, I'm sure, to solve our doubts and let us
                                        know . . .

COUNTRYMAN

Before you start your questioning
    come off that seat:
You're tresspassing on holy ground.

OEDIPUS

Holy ground? What god is sacred here?

COUNTRYMAN

It's untouchable—not to be inhabited—
    abode of most stern goddesses:
    daughters of Earth and Darkness.

OEDIPUS

Then let me pray to them. What are their holy names?

COUNTRYMAN

The All-seeing Eumenides or Kindly Ones, we call them
                                        here.
    In other places graced no doubt by other names.

OEDIPUS

Then let them welcome me, their suppliant,
   for I shall never set my foot outside this haven here.

COUNTRYMAN

What do you mean?

OEDIPUS

I recognize the signs—my journey's end.

COUNTRYMAN

Well, I've no power to shift you without a warrant.
I must go and let the city know.

OEDIPUS

Meanwhile, my friend, for the love of all the gods,
   don't disappoint a homeless wanderer, but tell me . . .

COUNTRYMAN

Ask. I have no call to disappoint.

OEDiPUS

Then where have we come to? Does this place have a
                 name?

COUNTRYMAN

I'll tell you everything I know.
This whole ground is sacred. Great Poseidon holds it.
Prometheus the Titan who bore fire is present here.
The very spot you occupy is called "The Brazen
                 Threshold,"
   the cornerstone of Athens.
That statue there, that horseman who rides above the
                 fields,
   is Colonus himself, origin and Lord of all this clan,

who gave the place its name:
Perhaps not much to sing about but, believe me Stranger,
living music to all who inhabit here.

OEDIPUS

So there are inhabitants in these parts?

COUNTRYMAN

Certainly, and called after their horseman hero there.

OEDIPUS

But who governs them? Or do they rule themselves?

COUNTRYMAN

A king in Athens rules over them.

OEDIPUS

A respected monarch whose word is law? Who is he?

COUNTRYMAN

His name is Theseus, son of King Aegeus before him.

OEDIPUS

Then could I send a message by one of you to him?

COUNTRYMAN

A message, what? Asking him to come?

OEDIPUS

To say, "a little favor wins a great reward."

COUNTRYMAN

Great reward? What can a blind man give?

OEDIPUS

You shall *see*—there's vision in every syllable I say.

COUNTRYMAN

Listen, stranger, I am out to help.
You are obviously well-born, though down in luck.
Stay where you are, exactly where I found you,
    while I go and tell the local people here.
Let *them* decide whether you are to stay or go.

[*The* COUNTRYMAN *hurries off*]

OEDIPUS

Daughter, has that person gone?

ANTIGONE

Gone, Father. Be at ease. Say anything you like.
There's no one here but me.

[OEDIPUS *staggers to his knees in an attitude of prayer.*
ANTIGONE *stands watching a few paces away*]

OEDIPUS

Great mistresses of terrifying mien,
    I salute you first on bended knee
    in this your sanctuary.
Harden not your hearts against me or Apollo,
    for even when he told my doom
    he foretold me too
    that after long journeys I should come
    to my journey's end
    at a faraway place of rest, a shelter
    at the seat of you the dreaded Holy Ones.
"There," he said,
    "you will close your life of sorrows,
With blessings on the land that harbors you
    and curses on the people who cast you out."
Certain signs, he said, would warn me of these things:

earthquakes, thunder, lightnings from Zeus.
I realize now
    some gentle spell from you
    has pulled my steps toward this grove.
How else could I have found you first
    and wandered here—
    I the sober and you the wineless ones—
To sit upon this holy seat not made with human hands?
Therefore, you kind divinities,
    in fulfillment of Apollo's prophecies,
    grant me here to reach my term at last,
    my rounding off of life;
Unless you think me far too vile for that—
    I a slave to sorrow far worse than any slave's.
So, hear me, good daughters of primeval Night.
And Athens, you first of cities, namesake of great Pallas,
    pity this poor remnant, Oedipus,
    this ghost, this carcass of what he was—a man.

ANTIGONE

Quiet, Father! Some elderly men are coming our way,
    spying out your resting place.

OEDIPUS

Then quiet I'll be,
    while you hurry me off this path into the grove,
    until I hear just what it is they have to say.
It's always wise to be informed before we act.

[OEDIPUS *and* ANTIGONE *hustle into the trees*]

FIRST CHORAL DIALOGUE

[*Enter the* CHORUS *of Elders of Colonus. They scurry about, searching among the bushes and behind the rocks, meanwhile uttering severally:*]

Strophe I

Look for him?
        Who is it?
               Where can he lurk?
Where has he bolted?
            Oh what a sacrilege!
Comb the ground.
      Strain your eyes.
         Search him out everywhere.
A vagabond, surely,
      some aged vagabond.
No one from here,
      would ever have pushed
Into this virgin plot of the unaffrontable maidens,
Whose very name sends shivers,
        whom we pass with averted eyes,
Whom we pray to with quavering lips.
But now a blasphemous rogue
       is hidden somewhere they say,
And I've covered the ground on every side
But still I cannot uncover
       the cranny in which he hides.

[OEDIPUS *and* ANTIGONE *step from the trees*]

OEDIPUS

I am the man and my ears are my eyes,
  as they say of the blind.

CHORUS

Ah! Horrible to see, and horrible to hear!

OEDIPUS

Listen, please! I am no criminal.

CHORUS

Zeus, defend us! Who could this old man be?

OEDIPUS

No favorite of fate—I can tell you that—
    good guardians of this grove.
For who would borrow eyes to walk,
    or lean his weight on frail support?

Antistrophe I

Look at his eyes!
            Great gods!
                    He's blind!
Eyeless from birth?
            What a lifetime of horror!
Far be it
    from us, sir,
            to add to your sorrows,
But you trespass, you trespass;
                    step no further
Into the still
    of the grassy dell
Where chaliced water from the spring, blended with
                                        honey,
Is poured in a stream of the purest offering. Go
Away from there, you woebegone stranger.
Turn back, come away,
    no matter how far you have wandered.
Can you hear us from there, you derelict outcast?
Speak if you want, and we'll listen, but not
    till you've moved from the sacred close.

[OEDIPUS *and* ANTIGONE *stand motionless*]

OEDIPUS

My daughter, what are we to do?

ANTIGONE

Do as they say, Father. We must yield and listen.

OEDIPUS

Your hand then, come.

ANTIGONE

There, you have it.

OEDIPUS

Sirs, I am breaking cover.
You must not violate my trust.

CHORUS

Never fear, old man!
No one will drag you off from here against your will.

[OEDIPUS *takes a step forward out of the grove. End of
strophic pattern but not of Choral Dialogue*]

OEDIPUS

Further?

CHORUS

Come still further.

[*He takes another step*]

OEDIPUS

Enough?

CHORUS

Lead him, girl, you understand.

ANTIGONE

I do indeed—these many years . . . Careful now!

OEDIPUS

Oh, what it is to walk in the dark!

ANTIGONE

Come, Father, come! Let your blind steps follow.

CHORUS

Poor harassed stranger on strange soil!
Learn to loathe what we find loathing.
Learn respect for what we reverence.

OEDIPUS

Then guide my walking, you my daughter,
Down the path of pious bidding
Where we can talk without offending.
Let's not fight with what is fated.

[*He advances onto a platform of rock at the edge of the grove*]

CHORUS

There.
You need not go beyond that ledge of rock.

OEDIPUS

This far?

CHORUS

That is far enough. Do you hear us?

OEDIPUS

May I sit?

CHORUS

Yes, sit to the side of that slab of rock.

ANTIGONE

I have you, Father. Lean on me.

OEDIPUS

Oh, what a wretched thing it is! . . .

ANTIGONE

Step by step, we together,
Old and young, weak and strong;
Lean your loving weight on mine.

OEDIPUS

Oh, how pitiable my wretchedness!

[ANTIGONE *finally settles him on the rock*]

CHORUS

You sad old man, relax at last
And tell us of your birth and home.
What prompts this weary pilgrimage?
What country are you from?

OEDIPUS

[*alarmed*]

Country? None. . . . Oh please, good friends, do not . . .

CHORUS

Do not what, old man? What are you avoiding?

OEDIPUS

Do not . . . Oh please—
   not ask me who I am!

CHORUS

Why? What is it?

OEDIPUS

My frightening origin.

CHORUS

Tell it.

OEDIPUS

[*turning to* ANTIGONE]
Dear child, must I out with it?

CHORUS

Sir, your ancestry? Your father's name?

OEDIPUS

No no, not that! Child, what shall I do?

ANTIGONE

Tell them, since you've gone so far already.

OEDIPUS

Then I'll say it. There's no way to cover up.

CHORUS

Both of you—you're wasting time—get on with it.

OEDIPUS

Laius . . . Have you heard the name?

CHORUS

Dear gods! We have.

OEDIPUS

Of the line of Labdacus?

CHORUS

Great Zeus!

OEDIPUS

And Oedipus the stricken one?

CHORUS

What! That man is you?

OEDIPUS

Wait, listen—do not recoil.

CHORUS

Oh monstrous! Monstrous!

OEDIPUS

It's hopeless now.

CHORUS

Intolerable!

OEDIPUS

Daughter, what will happen now?

CHORUS

Away with both of you! Leave our land!

OEDIPUS

But you promised! You will keep your word?

CHORUS

There is no blame attached to any
Who hits back where first he's wronged.
You deceived us, so we're playing

Trick for tricking, paying back
Treachery with trouble. Go!
Quit these precincts, quit our country,
Do not pollute our city with your tainted air.

ANTIGONE

You gentle sirs of pious intent,
If unmoved by my father's plight
And all those horrors not his fault,
To me at least be kind, who beg you.
He is my father, all I have.
I'm pleading with my eyes to yours:
Eyes not blind, but eye to eye,
Almost as if I were your daughter,
Beseeching you for a beaten man
Needing mercy. Like a god
You have us wholly in your hands.
Come, be clement past our hoping.
By all your dearest roots to life,
I implore you: child and wife,
Hearth and godhead. Bear in mind
There never was a human being
Who, god-impelled, had hope in fleeing.

[*End of Choral Dialogue*]

FIRST EPISODE

CHORUS

Daughter of Oedipus, of course we pity you,
　　just as we pity him for what he suffers;
But we dare not risk divine displeasure
　　and go beyond what we've said already.

OEDIPUS

Then where has fame and where has reputation gone
　　if this be Athens that most pious city?

Sanctuary of the lost, savior of the needy,
   unique in both! What good are they
When you tear me from my seat of stone
   and cast me headlong from the land?
And all because you've merely heard my name!
Me, this carcass, this right hand of mine,
   you can't fear that; for what I've done is simply suffer:
Yes, suffer much more than anything I've done.
As I could prove if I but touched upon the story
   of my mother and my father.
It's this that frightens you, as well I know.
Am I then a sinner born?
I, provoked to strike in self-defense?
Why, even if I'd acted with full knowledge,
   it still would not have been a crime.
As it was, where I went I went
All ignorant toward a doom too known
   to those who planned it.

Therefore, good sirs,
   since you have moved me from my seat,
   you must—by all the gods—protect me now.
Do not say you reverence heaven,
   then do nothing but ignore what heaven says.
Make no mistake,
   the gods' eyes see the just
   and the gods' eyes see the unjust too,
   and from that blazing gaze,
   never on this earth,
   will the wicked man escape by flight.
By heaven's grace then,
   let no dishonor blot the name of Athens by abeting
                             wrong.
You accepted me as suppliant and gave a pledge,
   now guard me to the end.
And when you look into my ruined eyes,
   do not look with scorn.

I am a priestly and a holy man,
   and come with blessings for your people in my hands.
And when your prince shall come,

whoever be your prince,
Then shall everything be told and all made plain.
But in that space between do nothing mean.

CHORUS

Your words, old man, must make us think.
These solemn arguments have weight.
Let authority decide. We are content.

OEDIPUS

And where is he who wields authority?

CHORUS

In Athens, our ancestral city.
The scout who sent us here has gone for him.

OEDIPUS

What hope is there that he will come?
Why should he trouble with a blind old man?

CHORUS

Certainly he will come—once he hears your name.

OEDIPUS

But who will tell him that?

CHORUS

The road is long but travelers talk.
He will hear your name and he will come.
For every region of the earth has heard your name, old
                                              man.
The instant that it hits his ears
    he will leap up from his recreation and his ease
    and hurry here.

OEDIPUS

Then may his coming bring rewards
    for myself and for his city.
Ah! Is not nobility its own reward?

ANTIGONE

Great heavens, I am speechless!
Father, I can't imagine it.

OEDIPUS

What's happening, Antigone, my child?

ANTIGONE

I see a woman coming straight toward us on a colt,
    an Etnan thoroughbred.
She wears a broad Thessalian hat
    to shade her from the sun.
I can't be sure. Is it she or isn't it?
Is my mind wandering? It can't be her . . . surely can it?
But it must be . . . It is.
Her eyes are flashing welcomes.
She's almost on us. She's waving now.
Of course . . . it's no one but our own Ismene.

OEDIPUS

What are you saying, child?

ANTIGONE ˙

That your daughter—and my sister—is right in front of
                                                    me.
Wait till you hear her voice.

[ISMENE, *attended by a single servant, advances toward*
OEDIPUS *and* ANTIGONE]

ISMENE

Dearest Father! Sister!
The sweetest names in the world to me.
It was difficult to find you, and now
  it's difficult to see you through my tears.

OEDIPUS

Darling daughter—you?

ISMENE

Poor dear Father!

OEDIPUS

But, child, you're really here?

ISMENE

It was not easy.

OEDIPUS

Dear girl—let me feel you.

ISMENE

Let me hug you both.

[*They all embrace*]

OEDIPUS

My children! . . . My sisters!

ISMENE

The stricken ones.

OEDIPUS

Yes, she and I.

ISMENE

With me the third.

OEDIPUS

But, Daughter, what has brought you?

ISMENE

Concern for you, Father.

OEDIPUS

You mean, you missed me?

ISMENE

Yes. And I've come with news,
   trusting myself to this last loyal servant here.

OEDIPUS

But those young men your brothers, where are they?

ISMENE

Just where they are—in the thick of trouble.

OEDIPUS

Oh, what miserable and perfect copies
   have they grown to be of Egyptian ways!
For there the men sit at home and weave
   while their wives go out to win the daily bread,
   as you do, my daughters.
Just so your brothers, who should be
   the very ones to take this load upon them.
Instead they sit at home like girls
   and keep the house,
   leaving the two of you to face my troubles
   and make life a little easier for me.
Antigone here,

ever since she left the nursery
and became a woman,
has been with me as guide and old man's nurse,
steering me through my dreary wanderings;
often roaming through the tangled forests,
barefoot and hungry,
often soaked by rain and scorched by sun,
never regretting all she'd missed at home,
so long as her father was provided for.

And you, my daughter,
more than once you've sallied forth
slipping past the Theban sentinels
to bring your father news of all the latest oracles.
You were my faithful spy
when I was driven from the land.
But, Ismene, what new tidings do you bring your father?
What mission has summoned you from home?
You don't come empty-handed, that I know.
You've brought me something—
something I can fear.

ISMENE

I went through fire and water, Father,
to find out where you were and how you were
surviving,
but let that pass;
I have no desire to live it all again
by telling you.

The trouble now is those two sons of yours
that's what I've come to tell you.
They were content at first to leave the throne to Creon,
and rid the city of the ancient family curse
that has dogged our line.
But now they are possessed.
Some demon of pride, some jealousy,
has gripped their souls
with a manic lust for royal power.

They want to seize the reins of government.
Eteocles, our hot-brained stripling younger brother,
   has snatched the throne from his elder, Polyneices,
   and driven him from Thebes.
While Polyneices, we hear from every source,
   has fled to the vale of Argos,
   adds marriage to diplomacy and military alliances,
And swears that Argos will either
   acquit herself with triumph on the Theban plain
   or be lifted to the skies in glorious attempt.
This is no fiction but the agonizing truth.
How far the gods will go before they let some mercy
                                    fall—

Oh, Father, fall on you!—it's impossible to tell.

OEDIPUS

Ah! Did you think that any glances of the gods
   could ever be a glance to save me?

ISMENE

Yes, Father, that I hoped, exactly that.
There've been new oracles.

OEDIPUS

My child, what oracles? What have they said?

ISMENE

That soon the men of Thebes will seek you out,
   dead or alive: a talisman for their salvation.

OEDIPUS

Ha! a talisman for what—one such as I?

ISMENE

In you, they say, there is a power born—a power for them.

OEDIPUS

So, when I am a nothing, then am I a man?

ISMENE

The gods now bear you up; before they cast you down.

OEDIPUS

An old man on a pedestal, his youth in ruins!

ISMENE

Nevertheless, this you ought to know.
Creon is on his way to use you, and sooner now than
later.

OEDIPUS

To use me, Daughter? How?

ISMENE

He wants to plant you on the frontiers of Thebes;
within their reach, of course, but not within their sight.

OEDIPUS

On the threshold, then? What use is that?

ISMENE

It saves them from a curse if your tomb be wronged.

OEDIPUS

But bestows a blessing if it is honored.
They needed neither god nor oracle to tell them that.

ISMENE

And so they want to keep you somewhere near,
but not where you can set up as master of yourself.

OEDIPUS

And when I die, to bury me in Theban dust at least?

ISMENE

No, dear Father, no: you spilled your father's blood.

OEDIPUS

Then I'll not fall into their hands—no, never!

ISMENE

And *that*, one day, will spell the ruin of Thebes.

OEDIPUS

How so, my child? What way will they be hurt?

ISMENE

Scorched by the anger blazing from your tomb.*

OEDIPUS

Who told you, child, all this you're telling me?

ISMENE

Pilgrims from the very hearth of Delphi.

OEDIPUS

And Apollo really said these things of me?

ISMENE

So those men avowed on their return to Thebes.

OEDIPUS

Has either of my sons heard this?

---

*This refers to the day when the Theban invaders of Athens will be routed in battle near the tomb of Oedipus.

ISMENE

Both of them alike; each taking it to heart.

OEDIPUS

Scoundrels! So they knew it! Coveted my presence less
than they coveted a crown.

ISMENE

It hurts to hear you say it, but it's true.

OEDIPUS

Oh you gods! Tread not down
the blaze of coming battle between these two.
And give me power to prophesy the end
for which they now match spear with clash on spear.

Then shall the one who now
enjoys the scepter and the throne
no more remain,
And he who fled the realm, not return.
I was their father,
thrust out from fatherland in full disgrace.
They did not rescue or defend me.
No, they cared nothing:
but watched me harried from my home,
my banishment proclaimed.
And if you say that such was then my wish,
a mercy granted by the city—apt and opportune—
I answer, "No!"
On that first day I wished it, yes,
death was sweet—my soul on fire—
even death by stoning,
but no man was found to further that desire.
In time my madness mellowed.
I began to think my rage had plunged too far,
my chastisement excessive for my sins.
And then the city—city, mark you, after all that time—
had me thrust and hurtled out of Thebes.

Then they could have helped,
  my two boys, their father's sons—
  then they could have stirred themselves.
They could. They did not do a thing.
For lack of a little word from them
  I was cast out
  to drag away my life in wandering beggary.
Shelter, devoted care, my daily bread,
  everything within a woman's power to give,
  these I owe to my two daughters here.
Their brothers sold their father for a throne,
  exchanged him for a scepter and a realm.

No, I'll not help them win a war,
And the crown of Thebes will prove to be their bane.
That much Ismene's oracles make clear
  now that I match them with those others,
  those olden oracles Apollo made me once
  and now at last fulfills.
So let them send a Creon to search me out;
  or any other potentate from Thebes.
I shall be your city's champion and the scourge
  of all my enemies,
With you, good people, on my side,
And by the grace of the Holy Ones who here abide.

CHORUS

Certainly, Oedipus, you impel our sympathies,
  you and your two daughters here.
And now that you add the sovereign weight
  of your great name to make our city triumph
  we are more than ready to help you with advice.

OEDIPUS

Good friends, I'll carry out whatever you suggest.

CHORUS

Then expiate at once those goddesses
  whose holy precincts you profaned.

OEDIPUS

By what ritual, friends? Tell me that.

CHORUS

First, from the spring of living waters fetch
  in pure washed hands the ceremonial draught.

OEDIPUS

And when I've fetched this fresh unsullied cup?

CHORUS

You'll find some chalices of delicate design.
Crown with wreaths their double handles and their
                                                brims.

OEDIPUS

What kind of wreaths? Olive sprigs or flocks of wool?

CHORUS

A ewe-lamb's fleece, all freshly shorn.

OEDIPUS

Good. And then, . . . How do I complete the rite?

CHORUS

Pour out your offering, with your face towards the dawn.

OEDIPUS

Pouring from those chalices you spoke of?

CHORUS

Yes, in three libations, emptying the last.

OEDIPUS

And this last, please tell me clearly:
  what should it contain?

CHORUS

Water mixed with honey. Add no wine.

OEDIPUS

And when the green-shadowed ground has drunk this
                                              cup?

CHORUS

Lay thrice nine sprigs of olive on it
  and with both hands offer up a prayer.

OEDIPUS

The Prayer? That's most important. Tell me that.

CHORUS

That these goddesses we call the Kindly Ones, or
                                      Eumenides,
  be saving kind to you, who pray to them.
Make that your prayer, or someone make it for you.
Whisper it and do not cry it out.
Then come away. Do not turn back.
This accomplished, we shall gladly stand by you;
  otherwise, my friend, we are afraid.

OEDIPUS

My daughters, did you hear what these locals said?

ANTIGONE

Father, we heard. Tell us what you want.

OEDIPUS

I cannot go. I am too weak and blind—
  my double disability.
Will one of you two do it for me?
A single person pure of heart, I think,
  can make atonement for a thousand sinners.
So do it now, but do not leave me all alone.
I am not strong enough to get along without a helping
                                             hand.

ISMENE

Then I shall carry out the rite,
  if somebody will point the way.

CHORUS

Beyond that clump of trees, young woman.
The guardian of the grove will tell you
  everything you want to know.

ISMENE

To my task, then.
Antigone, you watch over Father here.
No trouble is too much for a parent anywhere.

[ISMENE *goes into the grove. The* CHORUS *turns to*
OEDIPUS]

SECOND CHORAL DIALOGUE

Strophe I

CHORUS

Stranger it hurts
  to stir up the memory
    time has let slumber,
      but we must know . . .

OEDIPUS

What now?

CHORUS

The story of suffering
   you have been chained to:
      the fatal ordeal without a cure.

OEDIPUS

For hospitality's sake, my friends,
   do not uncover my shame.

CHORUS

The tale of it echoes
   all over the universe.
      But the truth of it, tell us,
         how much is true?

OEDIPUS

No! No!

CHORUS

We beg you tell.

OEDIPUS

Ah, the shame of it!

CHORUS

Grant us this favor
   as *we* favored *you*.

Antistrophe I

OEDIPUS

Friends, so many sufferings
   suffered unwittingly!
     God is my witness,
       none of it guiltily.

CHORUS

How did it happen?

OEDIPUS

An innocent bridegroom,
   a twisted wedding
     yoking Thebes to disaster.

CHORUS

Is there truth in the word that you shared
   the incestuous bed of a mother?

OEDIPUS

Must you, good people?
   It's death to hear it.
     Ah, these maidens are mine,
      but more than that . . .

CHORUS

Go on! Go on!

OEDIPUS

Two daughters, two curses . . .

CHORUS

Zeus, oh no!

OEDIPUS

Two shoots from the birthpangs
of a wife-mother's tree.

Strophe II

CHORUS

What! Are you saying, your children are both . . .

OEDIPUS

Their father's offspring and his sisters.

CHORUS

Horrible!

OEDIPUS

Horror, yes horror. Wave upon wave.

CHORUS

Victim!

OEDIPUS

Yes, endlessly victim.

CHORUS

Sinner, too!

OEDIPUS

No sinner.

CHORUS

How?

OEDIPUS

I saved
The city—I wish I had not—
And the prize for this has broken my heart.

Antistrophe II

CHORUS

Broken your heart with shedding the blood of . . . ?

OEDIPUS

What is it now? What more are you after?

CHORUS

A father . . .

OEDIPUS

Stab upon stab!
    wound upon wounding!

CHORUS

Killer!

OEDIPUS

I killed him, yes, but can plead . . .

CHORUS

What can you . . . ?

OEDIPUS

Justice.

CHORUS

How?

OEDIPUS

Let me tell you:
  The man that I murdered would have killed *me*.
By law I am innocent, void of all malice.

[*End of Choral Dialogue.* THESEUS *and his retinue are
seen approaching. The* CHORUS *turns in his direction*]

CHORUS

But here comes our king, Theseus son of Aegeus,
  bent upon your bidding.

[*Enter* THESEUS *with soldiers and attendants. He stands
gazing at* OEDIPUS]

THESEUS

That story noised abroad so often in the past,
  the bloody butchering of your sight,
  warned me it was you, Son of Laius,
And now, hastened here by rumors,
  I can see it is.
Your clothes, your mutilated face,
  assure me of your name.
And I would gently ask you, tortured Oedipus,
  what favor you would have of me or Athens:
You and that sad companion by your side?
Tell me.
For no tale of yours however shocking
  could make me turn away.
I was a child of exile too,
  fighting for my life in foreign lands—
  and none so dangerously.
So never could I turn my back on some poor exile
  such as you are now
  and leave him to his fate.
For I know too well that I am only man.
The portion of your days today
  could be no less than mine tomorrow.

OEDIPUS

Theseus, in so short a speech
   all your birth's declared,
   and my reply can be as brief.
My name, my father and my country,
   you've touched on all correctly.
There's nothing left for me to say
   but tell you my desire,
   and all my tale is told.

THESEUS

I wait to hear it. Please proceed to tell.

OEDIPUS

I come with a gift: this my battered body.
No priceless vision, no,
But the price of it is better than of beauty.

THESEUS

What makes it precious, this gift you bring?

OEDIPUS

In time you'll know. Not now perhaps.

THESEUS

And when will that time of grace be known?

OEDIPUS

When I am dead and you have raised my tomb.

THESEUS

Life's last rites, you ask for that,
   with all before made nothing of, forgotten!

OEDIPUS

Yes, for in that wish the rest is harvested.

THESEUS

You ask a little favor, then, compressing everything?

OEDIPUS

Perhaps, but not so little—believe me—not so little.

THESEUS

Does it, then, concern your sons and me?

OEDIPUS

It does, my king, they are intent to carry me off to
                                                Thebes.

THESEUS

Which ought to please you, surely, more than banishment?

OEDIPUS

No. For when I wanted that they would not have it.

THESEUS

This is foolishness to sulk in time of trouble.

OEDIPUS

Wait till you've heard me out before you scold.

THESEUS

Proceed. I have no right to judge before I know.

OEDIPUS

I am the victim, Theseus, of repeated and appalling
                                                wrong.

THESEUS

You mean the family curse that haunts your line?

OEDIPUS

No. *That* already rings in Greece's ears.

THESEUS

But what could be worse than that—
   the worst wretchedness of all?

OEDIPUS

Just this:
   I am driven from my native land by my own flesh and
                               blood.
   I can return no more. I am a parricide.

THESEUS

What, ostracized and summoned home in one?

OEDIPUS

The god has spoken. His warning makes them want me
                               there.

THESEUS

And what is the warning threatened by the oracle?

OEDIPUS

A mortal wound dealt on this very field of battle.

THESEUS

This field of battle? But Athens and Thebes are not at
                               war.

OEDIPUS

Good son of Aegeus, gentle son,
   only to the gods is given not to age or die,
All else disrupts through all disposing time.
Earth ebbs in strength, the body ebbs in power.
Faith dies and faithlessness is born.
No constant friendship breathes
   between man and man, or city and a city.
Soon or late, the sweet will sour,
   the sour will sweet to love again.
Does fair weather hold between this Thebes and you?
Then one day shall ever teeming time
   hatch nights on teeming days,
Wherein this pledge, this harmony, this hour
   will break upon a spear,
   slashed down for a useless word.

Then shall my sleeping corpse,
   cold in sepulcher,
   warm itself with draughts of their perfervid blood,
If Zeus is Zeus and truth be truth
   from Zeus's son Apollo.
But I'm not one to bawl away a mystery,
   so let me stop where I began:
Take care to keep your word with me,
   then never shall you say of Oedipus
   you gave him sanctuary without reward;
Or, if you do, all heaven is a fraud.

CHORUS

Sire, from the first this man has sworn
   he had the power to benefact our land.

THESEUS

How could we spurn the overtures of such a friend,
   who not only rightly claims the hospitality
   of Thebes an allied city,

But comes appealing to our goddesses
  and pays no little tribute to our State and me?
I shall reverence and not repudiate his gift
  and grant him all the rights of citizen.
But more: if it please our guest to sojourn here,
  I place him in your care.
  yes Oedipus—unless you'd rather come with me—
  the choice is yours,
  your every wish is mine.

OEDIPUS

Great Zeus, be gentle to such gentleness!

THESEUS

Well, what is your wish? Will you come with me?

OEDIPUS

If only that were fitting, but this very place is where I
                                          must . . .

THESEUS

Must what? I shall not hinder you.

OEDIPUS

. . . triumph over those who banished me.

THESEUS

And as you promised, shower blessings on us with your
presence?

OEDIPUS

Only if you keep your word to me.

THESEUS

Never doubt it. I am not one to play you false.

OEDIPUS

And I'll not make you swear it like a criminal.

THESEUS

An oath would be no surer than my word.

OEDIPUS

But how will you proceed if . . .

THESEUS

What now disturbs you?

OEDIPUS

Men will come.

THESEUS

And mine will see to them.

OEDIPUS

But if you leave me . . .

THESEUS

You need not tell me what to do.

OEDIPUS

The fear in my heart compels me.

THESEUS

And there is no fear in mine.

OEDIPUS

But the threats . . . you do not know . . .

THESEUS

I know only this:
That no one is going to kidnap you against my will.
Often bluff and bluster, threat and counterthreat
  can bully reason for a time,
But when the mind reseats itself
  disquiet vanishes.
These people who have shouted lustily
  for your abduction,
Will, I trust, run into a long and ruffled passage here.
Have confidence!
Apart from all my promises, has not Apollo
  charge of you within this hallowed ground?
And when I'm gone,
  my name's enough to keep you sound.

[THESEUS *leaves with his retinue. The* CHORUS *regroups and faces the audience to deliver a eulogy on Colonus and Athens*]

CHORAL ODE

Strophe I

Stranger, here
Is the land of the horse
Earth's fairest home
This silver hill Colonus.

Here the nightingale
Spills perennial sound
Lucent through the evergreen.

Here the wine-deep ivies creep
Through the god's untrodden bower
Heavy with the laurel berry.

Here there is a sunless quiet
Riven by no storm.
Here the corybantic foot
Of Bacchus beats
Tossing with the nymphs who nursed him.

Antistrophe I

The narcissus
That drinks sky's dew
Here lifts its day—
By-day-born eye:

The diadem that crowns
The curls of ancient goddesses.
The crocus casts his saffron glance

And unparched Cephisus all day
Wanders out from sleepless springs
Fingering his crystal way

Out among the gentle breasts
Of hills and dales
Swelling with fecundity.
Not seldom here the Muses sing
And Aphrodite rides with golden rein.

Strophe II

Not in Asia
Never in Pelops
(Great Dorian island)
Was heard the like of what I sing:
A tree indomitable, self-engendered,
Challenge to the spears of armies
Lush in Athens
Sap of striplings—
Olive, the moon-green olive.
No youth in lustihood
Shall ravish her
Nor calculating age.

The sleepless eye of Zeus is on her
Athena's gaze cerulean.

Antistrophe II

Add praise on praise:
Our mother city's
Prize and god-gift:
Prowess in horses, prowess in stallions
Prowess at sea. You Poseidon
Son of Cronus, sat her high,
Rode her down
These roads displaying
How the bit and bridle
Breaks the stamping charger
How the oarblade
Sleekly stroking
Cuts the brine behind
The hundred-footed Nereids.

SECOND EPISODE

[ANTIGONE's *attention is riveted by the approach of an old man hurrying toward them with a squad of soldiers*]

ANTIGONE

Look! You much praised land, the hour has come
   for you to make your words shine forth with deeds.

OEDIPUS

[*alarmed*]

Child, what now?

ANTIGONE

Creon is coming . . . And, Father, not alone.

OEDIPUS

You generous counselors, now is the time
to prove the limits of your sanctuary.

CHORUS

Take heart! Proof you'll have.
Though we be old, our country's strength is young.

[CREON *arrives at the head of his escort of guards*]

CREON

Sirs, you worthy men of Attica,
I see some apprehension in your eyes at my approach.
Do not recoil. Do not be ready with abuse.
I have not come to do you harm—
    an old man against a mighty state,
    mighty as ever there was in Greece.
My mission is to plead with that old man
    to return with me to Theban territory.
I am no private emissary—ah no!—
    but a nation's full ambassador.
It was my lot as this man's relative
    to bear the crushing load of his estate
    as no man else in Thebes.

[*He turns toward* OEDIPUS]

Do you hear me, Oedipus?
Come home you woebegotten man!
Everyone in Thebes is rightly calling for you;
    I most of all, yes, I,
    who'd be a brute indeed
    not to weep to see an old man suffer so:
    drifting endlessly, unknown, a vagabond,
    a girl his single prop—and she poor thwarted creature
Fallen lower than I'd ever dream she'd fall,
    dragging out her gloomy squalid life of caring for you:
    well ripe for weddings but unwed and waiting,
    ah! for some thick-fisted yokel's snatch.

A disgrace? Indeed, we are all disgraced.
I point at you and me and all of Thebes.
Who can cover up what so emblazons forth?
You can at last. Yes, Oedipus, you can hide it now.
By all our fathers' gods, consent to come back home,
    your own ancestral city.
Say farewell to Athens, kind as she has been.
Home comes first,
    the place of your long-gone cradlehood.

OEDIPUS

You brazen hypocrite! You'd stop at nothing.
Twisting every righteous motive to your ends!
You'd trap me, would you, in your cruel coils a second
                            time?
Once in agony I turned against myself
    and cried aloud for banishment.
Then it did not fit your pleasure, did it,
    to fit yourself to mine?
But when my overbrimming passion had gone down
    and home's four walls were sweet,
Then you had me routed out and cast away.
Fine affection *that* for family ties!

And now again, the moment you perceive
    me being welcomed by this kindly city and her sons,
    you want to wrench me away,
    your barbed designs wrapped up in words of wool.
Who ever heard of friendliness by force?
You're like a man who spurns to grant a favor when he's
                            asked,
    gives nothing, will not lift a finger for you,
Then when your heart's desire has passed,
    wants to push that very grace upon you,
    now a grace no longer.
Rather barren of delight that gift, do you not think?
Yet that precisely is the gift you proffer me,
    so fair in form, so hollow in reality.

Therefore, let me shout your falsehood out to these
   and let them gaze at your duplicity.
You come to fetch me—home? Ah no!
You come to plant me on your doorstep,
A talisman to ward away the onslaughts Attica will
                           launch.
That wish you'll never have, but this you will:
   my curse forever on your land,
And for my sons this sole realm and heritage—
   the right, and room enough, to die.
Ha! I'd say my forecast for the fate of Thebes
   was more informed than yours. Oh much!
   So much the more reliable!
It stems from Zeus and from Apollo.
Yours is from a counterfeiting tongue,
   double-edged and whetted to deceit.
But yours, you'll find, will reap more suffering than
                         success.
However, since I cannot make you see this—go!
And leave us here to lead a life of hardship as we may.
Hardship to those resigned is no dismay.

CREON

A splendid tirade!
But whom do you think it hurts, you or me?

OEDIPUS

What care I? So long as you fail as thoroughly
   to dupe these people here as you've duped me.

CREON

Silly obdurate man, whom time has not made wise!
Must you bring even dotage to disgrace?

OEDIPUS

Such a tricky tongue! I never knew an honest man
   who could dissertate and twist speech so.

CREON

Dissertation is quite different from frothing at the mouth.

OEDIPUS

You, of course, can dissertate and hit the bull's-eye
straight.

CREON

Not exactly straight—with such a crooked target.

OEDIPUS

Be off with you! I speak for all these people here.
I do not want you prowling round my haven.

CREON

Then I appeal to them, these people, not to you.
You I'll deal with once I've got you in my clutches.

OEDIPUS

Got me in your clutches, eh?
With these my friends all looking on?

CREON

Just wait! I know another way to make you wince.

OEDIPUS

Another way? I'd like to see exactly how.

CREON

Certainly! You have two daughters.
One I've already seized. The other will quickly follow.

OEDIPUS

Oh no!

CREON

Oh yes! And you'll soon have more to groan about.

OEDIPUS

You've got my child?

CREON

And soon will have the other.

OEDIPUS

Friends, my friends, is there nothing you can do?
You must not fail me now. Hound this horrible man
away.

CHORUS

Sir, be off with you! What you have done
and what you mean to do is criminal.

CREON

[*to his guards*]

Grab the girl. It's time to act.
Drag her off by force if she won't come.

[*The guards advance on* ANTIGONE]

ANTIGONE

Help! Is there no escape?
You gods! You men!

CHORUS

What are you doing, sirrah?

CREON

I shan't touch your man, but *she* is mine.

OEDIPUS

Elders, help!

CHORUS

Sir, you have no right.

CREON

I have indeed a right.

CHORUS

What right?

CREON

To take what's mine.

OEDIPUS

Men of Athens, help!

[CREON *lays hands on* ANTIGONE]

THIRD CHORAL DIALOGUE

[*The following lines form a strophe in the Greek which is answered later by an antistrophe when* CREON *attacks* OEDIPUS *himself. This short choral interlude serves both to sustain the excitement and yet to relieve the tension.*]

Strophe

CHORUS

[*approaching menacingly*]

How dare you, Stranger!
    Unhand her or you run the danger
    of our attack.

CREON

Stand back!

CHORUS

Not until you yield.

CREON

Then it's Thebes and Athens
  on the battlefield.

OEDIPUS

Ah! My prophecy come true!

CHORUS

Let loose the girl, or you . . .

CREON

Mind your own authority.

CHORUS

I'm telling you to set her free.

CREON

And I'm telling you to unbar my way.

CHORUS

Colonians, to the rescue! Help!
The State manhandled, the State itself at bay.

ANTIGONE

Friends! Friends! They're dragging me away.

[*End of strophe and of first part of Third Choral
Dialogue*]

OEDIPUS

Antigone, where are you?

ANTIGONE

They're dragging me away.

OEDIPUS

Hold on to my hand, child!

ANTIGONE

I haven't the strength.

CREON

[*to his guards*]

Get on with her!

OEDIPUS

This is the end of me.
[*The guards hustle* ANTIGONE *away.* CREON *pauses, then turns to* OEDIPUS *with a sneer*]

CREON

At least you won't go hobbling through your life
    with those two little crutches any more!
If that's the kind of triumph you want,
    trampling over friends and fatherland—
    those whose mandate I, as king,
    am trying to carry out—
Then *have* that triumph.
In time I think you'll learn
    you are your own worst enemy, before and now:
    flying into tantrums with your friends—
    those damnable tempers that have ruined you.

[CREON *begins to walk away, but realizes his men have gone off with* ANTIGONE *and he is now on his own, with his way blocked by the Athenian Elders*]

CHORUS

Hold there, Stranger!

CREON

Don't dare touch me!

CHORUS

Stay where you are till you restore those girls.

CREON

[*looking around and catching sight of* OEDIPUS, *who is backing into the grove*]

In that case I'll present my city with an even greater
prize
worth more than those two women.

[*He rounds on the retreating* OEDIPUS]

CHORUS

Whatever next?

CREON

Him. He's mine.

CHORUS

Braggart! You wouldn't dare.

CREON

Watch me do it!

CHORUS

Not if our sovereign king can stop you.

OEDIPUS

Villain, are you so far gone you'd even lay a hand on
me?

CREON

Hold your tongue!

OEDIPUS

That I will not.
If the hallowed spirits of this place allow,
 let me give vent to one more curse.
You scum! My devastated eyes, blank so long,
 saw through the eyes of this helpless girl
 and now you've plucked her from me.
So, may Helios, all-seeing god of sun,
 visit you and all your race
 with such dotage and decay as matches mine.

CREON

Do you hear him, men of Athens?

OEDIPUS

They hear all right. They mark you and me:
You the bully who use sheer force,
And I who can only counter with a curse.

CREON

[*advancing on* OEDIPUS]

I'll stand no more of this.
Old and single-handed though I am,
I'll take this man by the strength of my right arm.

[CREON *lays hands on* OEDIPUS *and attempts to drag him away*]

Antistrophe

[*matching the Strophe on page 135 and completing the Third Choral Dialogue*]

OEDIPUS

You'll rue it.

CHORUS

Rash man!
What makes you think that you can do it?

CREON

I can.

CHORUS

Then is Athens city most degenerate.

CREON

Where right is might the little beat the great.

OEDIPUS

Hear him?

CHORUS

Rant—Zeus knows!

CREON

Perhaps Zeus knows.

You don't and can't.

CHORUS

Unbridled insolence!

CREON

Then you'll have to bear unbridled insolence.

CHORUS

Rally, people! Rulers, rally!
To the rescue—hurry,
Before these ruffians cross our boundary.

[THESEUS *arrives at the head of a troop of men. End of antistrophe and of Third Choral Dialogue*]

THESEUS

What's all this clamor? What's going on?
Why was I called away by panic cries
    from Poseidon's altar, great sea-god of Colonus?
Explain it all,
    for I've hurried here much too quick for comfort.

OEDIPUS

Ah! welcome, gentle voice!
I am worsted by a brigand.

THESEUS

Worsted? How? Please tell me.

OEDIPUS

Creon here, this creature that you see,
    has kidnapped my two children,
    my last and darling pair.

THESEUS

Is this true?

OEDIPUS

As I tell it: the most foul truth.

THESEUS

[*to his men*]

Quick, one of you to the altar place.
Break up the concourse at the sacrifice
    and have the people gallop foot and horse
    to the meeting of the roads
    before the women pass:
Quick, off with you!
Before this foreign bully makes a fool of me by force.

[*A solider is dispatched.* THESEUS *turns to* CREON]

As for him,
    if I should let my anger have full sway
    to deal with him as he deserves,
    he'd not leave my hands without a smart.
We will, however, judge him by the very laws
    to which he himself appeals.

[*Pointing at* CREON]

You, you shall not leave this country, sir,
    until those girls are back and stand before my eyes.
You insult us;
    you insult your very race and native land.
You push your way within this realm
    where right is loved and law is paramount,
    and then proceed to sweep aside authority,
pillaging and taking prisoners at your will
    as if you thought my city was bereft of men
    or manned by slaves
    and I a nobody.
Well, it was not Thebes that brought you up to steal.
She has no predilection for a rascal brood.
Scant praise you'd have from her
    if she found you plundering me,
    plundering the gods,

carrying off by force
poor wretched victims come to plead.
Never could I see seize and snatch,
    entering territory of yours—
    not even if I had a more than royal right—
    unless whoever governed gave me leave for it.
I should know how a guest behaves on foreign soil.
But you, you dishonor your own city,
    so undeserving of disgrace.
Length of days has made you ripe in age
    but far from ripe in reason.
I have said it once, and I say it once again:
    restore those girls forthwith
    or you'll find your visit here prolonged by force—
    not quite according to your will.
    This is no idle talk. I mean it every syllable.

CHORUS

Stranger, see what you've brought upon yourself!
By birth and race you ought to know much better.

CREON

Theseus son of Aegeus,
    I never thought your city was unmanned by men
    or drifting rudderless, as you suggest.
That never prompted what I did.
No, I merely took for granted
    that your people here
    were never so devoted to my family
    as to harbor one of them against my will
    and welcome here
    a parricide,
    a tainted man,
    a man discovered—oh the filth of it!—
    both bridegroom and his own bride's son.
I took for granted that your famous Council
    on Ares' hill where Justice sits,
        would never in its wisdom let such reprobates

roam at large within your land.
Convinced of this, I hunted down my prize.
And even then I might have let him go
   had he not heaped on me and all my clan
   the foulest imprecations.
I've stomached quite enough, I think,
   to justify reprisals.
Rage, remember, knows no age till death.
Nothing hurts the dead.
Well, do what you will.
Though right is on my side,
   what headway can I make alone?
I may be old but I shall strain
   to counter every plan with counterplan.

OEDIPUS

Arrant monster!
On whom do you think these insults fall—
   on my old head or yours?
Murder, incest, deeds of horror,
   you spew the lot at me:
   and all the lot I bore in misery,
   not through any choice of mine
   but through some scheme of heaven,
   long incensed, it seems,
   against some misdeed of our line.
Examine me apart from this
   and you will find no flaw to cavil at
   that might have drawn me so to floor
   my family and myself.

For tell me this:
   Suppose my father by some oracle was doomed to die
   by his own son's hand,
   could you justly put the blame on me—
   a babe unborn,
   not yet begotten by a father,
   not yet engendered in a mother's womb?
And if when born—as born I was to tragedy—
   I met my father in a fight and killed him,

ignorant of what I did, to whom I did it,
can you still condemn an unwilled act?

And my mother, your own sister, wretched man . . .
    since you're low enough to drag her in
    and force me to allude to it, I shall.
I'll not keep silent when your own lewd mouth
has broken all the bonds of reticence. . . .
My mother, yes she was my mother—what a fate!
I did not know. She did not know.
And to her shame she gave me children,
    children to the son whom she herself had given.

One thing I know:
    you vituperate by choice, both her and me,
    when not by choice I wedded her,
    and not by choice am speaking now.
Neither in this marriage then
    shall I be called to blame,
    nor in the way my father died—
    which you keep casting in my teeth.

Let me ask you this, one simple question:
If at this moment someone
    should step up to murder you,
    would you, godly creature that you are,
    stop and say, "Excuse me, sir, are you my father?"
Or would you deal with him there and then?
Ah! You love your life enough, I think,
    to turn on him,
    not look around to find a warrant first.

That precisely was the plight that heaven put me in.
My father's very soul, come back, would not say no.
But you, the unscrupulous wretch you are,
A man convinced that everything he says is fit to hear,
    who bawls out every secret thing,
You heap your slanders on me publicly,
    meanwhile making sure to bow and scrape
    before the name of Theseus, with flattery
    and compliments on how the state of Athens runs.
Very well, extoll them to the skies but don't forget,

if there's any state that knows what true religion is,
that state is this.
And yet it was here you tried to wrest
a pleading worshipper away, an old man too,
and have taken captive both my daughters.
Therefore I rest my case before these goddesses,
lay siege to them in prayer,
assail them for their help
to fight for me, and manifest to you
the caliber of men that guard this realm.

CHORUS

Sire, this stranger is an upright man:
A woefully unlucky man and worthy of our aid.

THESEUS

Enough of talk!
The criminals are in full flight
while we stand still discussing it.

CREON

I am helpless then. What is it I must do?

THESEUS

My pleasure is
that you yourself shall show the way
and I shall escort you
to where the two missing girls are hidden.
But if your men have already hustled them away
we shall spare ourselves the trouble
and others will give chase and hunt your soldiers down,
and none shall escape to thank their gods at home.

All right, lead off! And bear in mind,
the looter has been looted,
the trapper's in the trap,
and stolen goods soon spoil.

Expect no help from your accomplice either.
Oh yes, I'm well aware
  you did not push yourself
  to this pinnacle of daring,
  this reckless outrage,
  without some help or backing.
And I must look to it,
    not jeopardize my city for a single man,
Does this make sense?
Or do my warnings seem to you as vain
  as any scruples when you hatched your plan?

CREON

I shall not argue with you on your own terrain.
But once at home, I'll have my inspirations too.

THESEUS

Threaten away, but keep moving please.
Oedipus, stay here in peace.
Rest happy in the pledge I give:
  I'll have your daughters back, or I'll not live.

OEDIPUS

Bless you, Theseus, for your nobility;
  bless you for your loving care of me.

[CREON *is marched off by* THESEUS *and his men*]

SECOND CHORAL ODE

[*In a galloping meter, the Elders excitedly follow the chase
in imagination, alluding to some of the most religiously
evocative centers dear to Athens, notably Apollo's oracle
at Delphi and Demeter's mystery-fraught shrine by the sea
at Eleusis. They also appeal to Pallas Athena, patroness
of Athens, to Poseidon, patron of horses and ships, to*

Apollo the supreme archer, and to his sister Artemis, the
supreme huntress.]

Strophe I

Oh to be there
      when the brigands at bay
Turn to the clash
      of bronze on bronze
Down by the Pythian shore
Or the flaring sands
      of Eleusis where
The Queens of the Night
      and their honey-voiced hymners
Solemnly seal
      in tongues of gold
The rites that bring blessings to man.

Ah! I think Theseus
      springs to the fight
With presage of victory
      strong in his shout
Soon to make safe
      two sisterly captives
Still in our land.

Antistrophe I

Or perhaps galloping
      onward they go
To the western plains
      past rocky Oéa's
Glens and snowblanched sides.
Neck and neck in the race
      chariots flying
Till Creon is worsted
      by terrible Ares
And by Theseus'
      stalwart men.

Ah, flash of the harness,
       toss of the reins!
Thunder of chargers,
       body of horsemen
Dear to Athena,
       Queen of the horse,
Dear to Poseidon Ocean embracer
       fond son of Rhea.

Strophe II

The tussle is on
       Or just to begin
A beautiful hope
       tells us that soon
The two young women
       are here returned,
Cornered so cruelly
       by an uncle so cruel.
Victory! Victory!
       Zeus win the day!
Success in the struggle
       is what I foretell.
Oh that my eyes—
       high over the battle—
Were the eyes of a dove
       that sails down the storm
And lifts to the passing cloud.

Antistrophe II

All-seeing Zeus,
       all-ruling all,
Let this country's
       guardians conquer.
Let them capture
       quarry and prize.
Grant, oh grant it!
       Your daughter too,

Pallas Athena,
> Our Lady stern.
Grant it Apollo!
> Hunter who
Beside his sister
> Artemis chases
The light-footed moon-speckled
> deer. Oh come!
Twin allies of this land and people.

[*As the strains of the Choral Ode die away, a member of the* CHORUS *hurries back with a report*]

THIRD EPISODE

CHORUS MEMBER

Wanderer, look!
The forecast of our watchers was not false,
for I see the girls returning under escort.

OEDIPUS

Where, where? What are you saying? . . .

[ANTIGONE *and* ISMENE *are led in by* THESEUS *and his soldiers.* ANTIGONE *runs forward*]

ANTIGONE

Father, Father!
I wish some god could give you eyes to see
> this princely man who has brought us back to you.

OEDIPUS

My child—it's you? Ah, both of you!

ANTIGONE

Both of us, saved by his strong arm:
  by Theseus and his gallant men.

OEDIPUS

Come to me, dear girls.
Let your father press you to his embrace—
  redeemed beyond all hope.

ANTIGONE

Beyond all hope! We could not ask for more.

OEDIPUS

But where—where are you?

ANTIGONE

Both here—hand in hand.

OEDIPUS

My own sweet darlings!

ANTIGONE

A father's favorites!

OEDIPUS

Dear props of my life!

ANTIGONE

And partners in pain.

OEDIPUS

My precious ones—ah, mine again!
If now I died they would not say
  he was altogether damned:
  he had his daughters with him in the end.

Press closer to me, each of you,
  don't let your father go.
Rest there from your late roaming
  so cruel and so forlorn
  and tell me in a word what happened:
  young girls need no speeches.

ANTIGONE

Father, our rescuer is here.
You should learn it all from him.
The credit is his.
There—my speech was short!

OEDIPUS

[*turning to where he thinks* THESEUS *is*]

Sir, forgive me!
I cannot welcome them enough.
My children were lost. Now they are found.
And you are the one who brings this joy to me:
You rescued them, no man else besides.
The gods reward you far beyond my dreams:
  reward-you and this blessed land
  where more than any other place on earth,
  among your people, I have found
Reverence and honesty and lips that cannot lie.
These things I recognize and pay my homage to.
All that I have, I have through you and no man else.
Therefore, my king, give me your hand and let me touch
                                                    it.
And let me put a kiss upon your cheek.

[*He takes a step toward* THESEUS, *then checks himself*]

What am I saying?
What is this invitation that I make
  to handle me a man of sorrows, a temple of pollution?
No, no! Never let it be; even if you would!
Let my sufferings lodge with those tried souls

who have drunk with me the bitter cup.
I salute you from afar.
Keep me always in your gentle care,
 as until this hour you have.

THESEUS

No, Oedipus, this is nothing strange:
Your shower of words, your open heart, your joy.
Of course you had to greet your children first.
How could *that* fill me with dismay?
Besides, I'd rather furbish life with sparkling deeds than
 words,
 as I have proved to you, good reverend sir,
 making perfect everything I pledged:
 presenting you with daughters both redeemed,
 rescued from all menaces.
As to the manner of my victory,
 why should I enlarge on that?
They will tell you everything.
Meanwhile, some late news has come my way
 and I should like your thoughts on it.
It hardly sounds to me important,
 and yet it puzzles me.
There's nothing that a wise man should dismiss.

OEDIPUS

What is it, son of Aegeus?
No news of anything has come to us.

THESEUS

They say a man, not from Thebes
 and yet a relative of yours,
 has unexpectedly appeared;
 is prone in prayer before Poseidon's altar,
Where I was worshiping before I started here.

OEDIPUS

A man from where?
And what is his petition?

THESEUS

I only know he wants a word with you,
    which will not cost you much.

OEDIPUS

Only a word, yet prostrate in petition?

THESEUS

Yes, he only wants to speak with you, they say,
    then go his way in peace.

OEDIPUS

Who can this be, praying at the shrine?

THESEUS

Think of Argos, have you any kinsman there
    who might ask a like request?

OEDIPUS

[*alarmed*]
Dear friend, do not go on!

THESEUS

Why? What's the matter now?

OEDIPUS

Don't ask.

THESEUS

Don't ask you what? Explain.

OEDIPUS

Argos, you said. I know now who it is.

THESEUS

Someone I must hold at bay?

OEDIPUS

Sire, my son, my own detested son.
There's no man's voice I find so poisonous.

THESEUS

Give him a hearing at least.
If you don't like what he asks, you needn't grant it.
Where's the pain in that?

OEDIPUS

Hate, my king! Though he *is* my son.
Do not press me to give way.

THESEUS

I think you must. The man has come to plead.
You must not fail in reverence to the god.

ANTIGONE

Father, listen to me, young though I am.
Let the king's desire be honored
    and his conscience satisfied
        to give the gods their due.
And for our sakes too, let our brother come.
After all, whatever pain his words may give,
    he cannot wrench your will away.
 And the sound of his voice—what damage can that do?
Besides, it's talk that best betrays the foul design.
You are his father,
And even if his conduct plumbed the depths of

wickedness,
that would never make it right for you, dear Father,
to pay him back in kind.
So let him come!
Many a man is pricked to anger by a renegade son
    but yielding to advice more reasonable and loving,
    is coaxed from harshness back to gentleness.

Cast your thoughts on what has been,
    not what is now:
All that your own father and mother caused you to
                                        endure.
Ponder this, and the lesson that it teaches:
    catastrophic anger brings catastrophe.
Think no further
    than those two sightless sockets once your eyes.
Come, give way to us!
We should not have to plead for a cause so fair.
Can one who has just felt mercy's touch
Then turn his back, not give as much?

OEDIPUS

Daughter, a hard-won joy you wring from me.
Well, have it as you wish.

[*He turns to* THESEUS]

But, oh my friend, that man—if he must come—
    never let him put me in his power.

THESEUS

Enough! I've told you once, old man,
    no need to ask again;
    nor shall I brag. But be sure of this:
Your life is safe while any god saves mine.

[THESEUS *departs with some of his soldiers, leaving a contingent to guard* OEDIPUS]

THIRD CHORAL ODE

[*The Elders, shaken by the wrangling and frustrations of two old men, dwell on the tragedy of life and the hopelessness of old age. The heavy trochaic and iambic beat measures out the sadness.*]

Strophe I

Where is the man who wants
More length of days?
Oh cry it out.
There is a fool
His dawdling years
Are loaded down
His joys are flown
His extra time but trickles on
He awaits the Comforter
Who comes to all.
No wedding march
No dancing song:
A sudden vista down stark avenues
To Hades realms,
Then death at last.

Antistrophe I

Not to be born has no compare
But if you are
Then hurry hence
For after that there is no better blessing.
When one has watched gay youth
Pack up his gallant gear
Vexations crowd without
And worries crowd within:
Envy, discord, struggles,
Shambles after battles
Till at last he too must have his turn
Of age, discredited and doddering:

Disaffected and deserted age
Confined with crabbedness
And every dismal thing.

Epode

So are we senile—he and I:
Lashed from the north by wintry waves
Like some spume-driven cape on every side
Lashed by our agonies those constant waves
Breaking in from the setting sun
Breaking in from the dawn
Breaking in from the glare of noon
Breaking in from Polar gloom.

FOURTH EPISODE

ANTIGONE

Father, I think I see our visitor approach.
He is alone. Tears are streaming from his eyes.

OEDIPUS

And who is he?

ANTIGONE

Exactly whom we thought.
It's Polyneices who has come.

[POLYNEICES *enters, advances, and stares aghast at his father and sisters*]

POLYNEICES

Oh my sisters, I'm at a loss!
Shall I pour out tears for my own calamities
   or for this sorry sight—my decrepit father?

Just look at him:
    jettisoned with two poor girls
    in an alien land;
    arrayed in such unkempt and antique filth
    his own antiquity corrodes with it:
    his hair above his sightless eyes
    straggling out upon the breeze;
    and matching this, his beggars scrip
    with pittance for his wasted belly.

Ah, too late! I see it all too late.
I pronounce that this neglect of you
    brands me as the most delinquent thing on earth.
Yes, let me be the first to say it.
But, Father,
    Zeus himself sits mercy by his throne,
    so may you seat her near you too.
We can mend mistakes and not make more.

[*He pauses anxiously*]

You are silent.
Say something, Father, please.
Don't turn away from me.
Have you no reply?
Will you send me off in mute contempt?
Not even tell me what upsets you so?

[*He pauses again*]

You his daughters, my own sisters, please,
    try to move him from this dumb rigidity.
I must not be dismissed in shame
    without a word of hope
    from this blessed seat of appeal—
    the god's own sanctuary.

[OEDIPUS *turns his back.* ANTIGONE *steps toward* POLY-
NEICES *and touches his arm*]

ANTIGONE

Tell him yourself, my stricken brother,
   why it is you came.
Sometimes as words begin to flow,
   here they strike a spark of joy,
     there they fan up anger or bring a touch of tenderness,
And anyhow, to the tongue-tied somehow give a tongue.

POLYNEICES

Then I'll speak out, for you advise me well.
But first let me make it plain,
   the god I've called on for his help
   is that very ocean god, Poseidon,
   from whose suppliant shrine this country's king
   has just now raised me up and let me come
   with safe conduct to confer with you.
Therefore I would ask you gentlemen,
   my sisters here, and you my father,
   to respect my rights in this.

And now I'll tell you, Father, why I came.
I am driven out, banished from my native land
   because as eldest son
   I claimed my sovereign birthright to your throne.
But Eteocles my younger brother has cast me out:
   not by making good his claims,
   nor by proof of excellence,
   but by cajoling the city to his side.
It all seems part of the curse that dogs your line,
   and this the various oracles confirm.
So I went to Argos in the land of Doria,
There took to wife the daughter of the king, Adrastus,
   and made a league
   of all the famous fighters of the Peloponnese
   to raise a seven-headed army aimed at Thebes
   and oust those from the realm who ousted me,
   or die in the attempt—die gloriously.

Well then, what is my point in coming here?

To petition, Father:
  to lay our supplications at your feet,
  mine and all my allies,
Who at this moment raise the standard of their seven
                                         spears
  and ring their seven armies round the plain of Thebes.
There's Amphiaraus, the hurricane spearsman,
  first at the spear, first at the reading of riddles.
Then the son of Oeneus: Tydeus of Aetolia.
Third comes Eteoclus, native of Argos.
Fourth, Hippomedon, sent by his father Talaus.
Fifthly Capaneus, swearing to mow down Thebes with
                                     fire.
Sixthly Parthenopaeus, born in Arcadia, son of Atalanta,
  that ferocious virgin who finally wedded
  and became the mother of this stalwart boy.
And lastly, I, your son,
  or if not your son
  but the child of some appalling fate,
  then son at least in name.
I am the one who puts this fearless Argos in the field
  against the state of Thebes.

Father, will you listen to us, to all of us:
  we beg you for your daughters' and your own life's
                                     sake.
Ease the harshness of your rage against me now:
I who sally out to give this wretched brother
                               chastisement,
  the one who thrust me out and robbed me of my
                               home.

If there's any truth in prophecy,
  the oracles have said
  that victory lies with those
  who win you to their side.
So listen, Father,
  if you love our land
  with its springing fountains,
  its Theban deities.
Be persuaded by my prayers.

We are exiles, you and I,
  both of us are beggars.
We have to fawn on others for a home, you and I,
  both share a single destiny.
And all the time
  this creature kings it in our house.
Insufferable!
He ridicules us from his cushioned pride.
If you will only bless my scheme,
  I'll make short shrift of him and scatter him.
I'll bring you home again and re-establish you,
  and I shall be established too.
I'll make good this boast, if you make one with me.
I shall not live, if you'll not now agree.

CHORUS

Oedipus, for Theseus' sake who sent him here,
  you must not let him go without some reasonable
                                           reply.

OEDIPUS

You trustees of this realm,
  since Theseus sent him here
  and asked me to reply, I will.
Nothing less would let him hear my voice.
But now he shall be graced with it
  in accents that will bring him little joy.

[*He turns toward* POLYNEICES]

Liar!
When you held the scepter and the throne
  which your brother at the moment holds in Thebes,
  you drove me out,
  drove this your father out,
  displaced me from my city.
You are the reason for these rags—
  rags that make you cry to see,
  now that you have reached rock bottom too.

The season for condolences is past.
What I must bear must last as long as life,
   last in my thoughts of you as my destroyer.
Oh yes, it's you that dragged me down!
You expelled me, you arranged
   that I should beg my daily bread.
But for my two girls
   I should not even be alive if left to you.
It's they who tend me, they preserve me.
They are the ones who play a man's and not a woman's
                        part.

But you, you and your brother—bastards—
   are no sons of mine.

The eye of Fate is on you now.
Her glance is mild to what it soon shall be
   if once your armies march on Thebes.
Never shall you topple down that city.
Instead, you'll trip up headlong into blood,
   your brother too,
   spattering each other.
Long ago I cursed you both,
   and now once more I summon up those curses,
   let them battle for me.
Let them teach you reverence
   for those that gave you birth.
Let them teach you what contempt is worth
   of an eyeless Father
   who had such worthless sons.

My daughters did not treat me so.
Therefore, if Justice is still seated
   side by side with Zeus
   in ancient and eternal sway,
I consign to perdition
   your sanctimonious supplications
   and your precious throne.
So, leave my sight. Get gone and die:
   you trash—no son of mine.

Die,
  with these my curses
  ringing in your ears:
Never to flatten your motherland beneath your spear,
Never to set foot again in Argive's vales,
Instead you die,
  die by a brother's blow
  and make him dead by yours
  who drove you out.

That's my prayer for you.
I summon the pitchy gloom of Tartarus
  to gulp you down
  to a new paternal home.
I summon the holy spirits of this place.
I summon Ares the Destroyer,
  who whirled you into hatred and collision.
With these imprecations in your ears, get out.
Go publish them in Thebes.
Go tell your bellicose and trusty champions
  the will and testament
That Oedipus bequeaths to his two sons.

CHORUS

Polyneices,
  Never have your missions boded peace,
  nor do they now.
Go as quickly as you can.

POLYNEICES

How pitiful!
My pointless journey here!
My hopes in ruins!
My comrades all betrayed!
What an end
  to our proud marching out from Argos town!

And none of this dare I whisper to my allies
   to try to turn them back.
I cannot halt them in the silent march to doom.

[*He turns to* ANTIGONE *and* ISMENE]

But you, his little ones, my sisters,
   now you've heard our father's prayers,
   his prayers of hate, please,
If ever they should come to bear their mortal fruit,
   and you be found in Thebes again,
Then by all the gods,
   on that blessed chance, I beg:
   do not let my shade be damned
   but put me in the tomb with hallowed rites.
So shall you earn more praises from me dead
   than from that living father
   for all you did.

ANTIGONE

Polyneices, wait. One thing I ask.

POLYNEICES

Antigone, sweet sister, what?

ANTIGONE

Turn your army back to Argos now.
Do not destroy yourself and Thebes.

POLYNEICES

Impossible! Once seen to flinch
   how could I put an army in the field again?

ANTIGONE

Again, my little brother?
What new madness could ever make you want to?
What can ruin of your native city gain?

POLYNEICES

Yes, but running from a younger brother,
  a laughingstock . . .

ANTIGONE

Ah, don't you see
  you'll make your father's prophecies come true:
  a duel to the death—
  the death of both of you?

POLYNEICES

That's what he wants. But I'll *not* give way.

ANTIGONE

Oh, I'm sick at heart!
And who will follow you once it's heard
  the future he has threatened?

POLYNEICES

It shan't be heard. I'll never say.
Good generals do not stress their weakness
  but their strength.

ANTIGONE

Your mind's made up? My poor misguided boy!

[*She throws her arms around him*]

POLYNEICES

It is. So do not try to hold me back.
There is an avenue down which I go
  beckoned by my father's prayers
  and dark with Furies answering his call.
May Zeus reward you both
  for the obsequies you do for me
  when I am dead.
In life there's nothing left

  for you to tender me,
Now let me go. Good-bye!
You'll never gaze again into my living eye.

[*He gently releases himself from* ANTIGONE]

ANTIGONE

[*breaking down*]

It breaks my heart!

POLYNEICES

Don't cry for me.

ANTIGONE

Oh, Polyneices, who would not cry to see
  you my brother hurrying to die?

POLYNEICES

If die I must, I'll die.

ANTIGONE

No, hear me—never you!

POLYNEICES

Don't press me uselessly.

ANTIGONE

Bereft of you, what is left for me?

POLYNEICES

The future is in Fortune's hands
  whether we live or die.
My prayer for both of you is this:
  Heaven keep you from every harm.
  You deserve none. As all affirm.

[*It would be characteristic of* ISMENE, *who has remained silent all this time, to have been rendered speechless by her tears. She too now advances and clings to her brother in a last farewell. After a moment,* POLYNEICES *disengages himself and strides away. The blind* OEDIPUS *has been standing by, mute as a stone*]

CHORAL ODE AND DIALOGUE

Strophe I

CHORUS

So do we see fresh sorrows strike
Fresh strokes of leaden doom
From the old blind visitor
Or is it Fate unfolding—
Supernal in her workings which
I dare not say can fail—
Watched, yes watched,
By never failing Time
Shuffling fortunes from the top to bottom?

[*A clap of thunder*]

The sky is rift. Great Zeus defend us!

OEDIPUS

Quick, children, oh my children,
    send someone to bring Theseus here,
    that princely man.

ANTIGONE

Father, what should make you call him now?

OEDIPUS

That clap of thunder beating down from Zeus
  beckons me to Hades realms.
So hurry, someone, hurry!

[*Another peal of thunder, followed by lightning*]

Antistrophe I

CHORUS

Louder—hear it?—crashing down
Divine report, dumbstriking sound
Pricking up my hair with panic
And shattering my soul.
There again! Light rips the sky
I'm stricken to the core with fear.
Such a pregnant rush of light
Never comes without some meaning
Never not with monstrous issue
Great awful sky! Great Zeus, oh, save us!

[*More thunder and lightning*]

OEDIPUS

Dear children, life is closing on me now:
  that predestined end from which there is no turning.

ANTIGONE

What makes you know? What signals do you have?

OEDIPUS

I am too well aware.
Oh hurry to this country's king
  and fetch him here.

[*More thunder*]

Strophe II

CHORUS

Ha! again, another crack
　　　shatters the air.
Come gently you powers, oh gently come
　　　if you must darken
This earth our mother. Show us some pity
　　　show us some clemency.
Though we have favored a stricken man
　　　hounded by destiny
　　Zeus, our king, be kind!

OEDIPUS

Daughters, is he here yet?
Shall I be breathing still?
Still master of my mind?

ANTIGONE

What is so urgent on your mind to tell him?

OEDIPUS

The crowning gift I promised in return.
The blessing to repay him for all he's done.

[*More thunder and lightning*]

Antistrophe II

CHORUS

Hurry, Theseus, my son, step down
　　　from altar and sacrifice:
Even from worship in the deep of the grove
　　　at Poseidon's shrine.
Don't tarry, don't linger, oh King, for the stranger
　　　brings city and people
A grace to reward you, a sovereign blessing
　　　for all you have done.
　　Theseus, Lord, come quickly!

[*With another peal of thunder and lightning,* THESEUS
bursts in]

THESEUS

What another summons?
Guest and people joined
In general clamor!
Bolts from Zeus
And catapults of hail!
All's possible when God
Hurls down such a storm.

[*End of Choral Ode and Dialogue*]

OEDIPUS

King, how glad I am to see you come!
Some god has surely smoothed your way to us.

THESEUS

What is it now, son of Laius?

OEDIPUS

The balance of my life is tilting.
    I must not die a debtor:
    my bargain barren still
    with you and with your city.

THESEUS

What signs declare to you the end is near?

OEDIPUS

This rolling thunder rolled,
    this shuttled light.
The fulminating bolts
    of unanswerable artillery.

THESEUS

And I believe.
You never did foreshadow falsely.
Declare what we must do.

[*With great solemnity,* OEDIPUS *draws* THESEUS *aside*]

OEDIPUS

Come, listen, son of Aegeus.
I lay before you now a city's lasting treasure.
There is a place where I must die.
And I myself unhelped shall walk before you there.
That place you must not tell to any living being:
   not where it lurks, not where the region lies,
   if you would have a shield like a thousand shields
   and a more perpetual pact than the spears of allies.

No chart of words shall mark that mystery.
Alone you'll go, alone your memory
   shall frame the spot.
For not to any person here,
   not even to my daughters so beloved,
   am I allowed to utter it.
You yourself must guard it always.
And when your life is drawing to its close,
   divulge it to your heir alone
   and he in turn to his, and so forever.

This way you will keep your city safe
   against the Dragon's seed, the men of Thebes,
   though many a state attack a peaceful home,
   though sure be the help from heaven (but exceeding
                        slow)
   against earth's godless men and men gone mad.
Be far from you such fate, good son of Aegeus!
But all this you know without my telling you.

[OEDIPUS's *face lights up as if inspired. With slow firm steps he moves forward*]

Now to that spot. The god within me calls.
Let us go forward and linger here no more.
Come beloved daughters, follow!
Follow this new leader guiding you:
  the father once you guided.

[ANTIGONE *and* ISMENE *attempt to assist him*]

No no, hands off! Let me walk my way
  without a prop toward my holy hidden tomb
  where the promised earth of Attica will cover me.
This way, this way—come!
For this way Hermes beckons me,
  and Persephone, mistress of the dead.

[*He turns his blind eyes up toward the sun*]

Farewell! Farewell! You blindfold light
  once light of mine,
  last vision felt in darkness.
I walk to Hades now
  to close my life in shade.

[*Turning to* THESEUS]

Most gentle friend,
  heaven bless you, bless your land and yours.
And in prosperity remember me, the dead,
That every grace abiding be ever on your head.

[OEDIPUS *moves slowly into the grove, followed by* THES-
EUS, ANTIGONE, *and* ISMENE. *The* CHORUS *watches until
they are out of sight*]

FOURTH CHORAL ODE

[*The* CHORUS *sings a "Requiescat in pace"* addressed to
Persephone and Hades, the queen and king of the underworld, and also to the Furies. Even Cerberus, the fierce*

---

*Let him rest in peace (as from the requiem mass).

three-headed hound that guards the portals of the dead,
is not left out of their appeal.]

Strophe

Dare we adore the unseen Queen
And you night's children's King?
Then Aidoneus, listen, Aidoneus:
Not in pain and lamentation
May his deathknell ring—
This stranger passing down
Through pallisades of gloom
Toward those prairies of the dead
   His stygian home.
   Much did he suffer
   much beyond deserts
Let the finger of God's fairness
   Raise him now.

Antistrophe

You goddesses or worlds deep down
And you untamed hulk of snarling hound
Watching, they say, the gates of hell
For those arriving at the gaping maw
Of Hades pit . . . Oh let him pass.
And Death you son of Earth and Tartarus
Muzzle the cur, so Cerberus
Shall not molest the lonely path
   Of Oedipus, who walks
   Toward those sunken
   Meadows of the dead
O Death bestow on him eternally
   Eternal rest.

[*After a pause, a* MESSENGER *appears at the entrance of
the grove*]

FIFTH EPISODE

Exodos

MESSENGER

Fellow citizens,
I could cut this story short and say:
  "Oedipus is gone,"
But what was done was not done shortly,
  and my story breaks away from brevity.

CHORUS

So the man of destiny has gone?

MESSENGER

Gone. He has left this life behind.

CHORUS

But did he have a blest demise all free from pain?

MESSENGER

It was extraordinary, most marvelous.
You yourselves saw how he went:
  unled by those he loved but walking on
  and showing us the way.
And when he'd reached that yawning orifice
  where steps of brass sink rooting down,
  he halted by the many branching ways
  where Theseus is remembered for his famous pact
  with Peiritheus to raid the underworld
  and bring Persephone back. And there,
  he stood at the chasm
Halfway between that basin and the slab of Thoricus,
By the old wild pear tree's hollow trunk and the marble
                         tomb.

Then sitting down he undid his squalid dress,
   and calling for his daughters bade them fetch
   water to wash with from the spring
   and some to pour in ritual for the dead.

So the women went to Demeter's hill in front of them
   (that goddess of unfolding spring),
   and soon had done all their father had enjoined;
 Then bathed and tended him and dressed him fittingly.
And when he was content that all was done,
   with nothing further he could wish,
   there came a grumbling sound from Zeus's underworld.
It shook the girls with trembling and they fell
   weeping at their father's knees.
 Nor would they stop but beat their breasts and sobbed.
And when he heard this bitter burst of grief,
   he took them in his arms and said:
   "This day, my daughters,
   you shall have no father left to you,
For all my life is done,
   your double burden of me done.
It was not easy, children, *that* I know,
   and yet one little word can change all pain:
That word is LOVE, and love you've had from me
   more than any man can ever give.
But now you must live on, when I am gone."

So did the three of them cling to one another
   calling out and crying
   until at last they came to the end of tears,
   and sobs gave out and all was still.

Then in that stillness suddenly a voice was heard,
   terrifying: their hair stood up with fear.
The voice of the god it was, calling out and calling:
   "Oedipus, Oedipus, why do we delay?
   You stay too long—too long you stay."
And when he knew it was the god that called,
   he craved King Theseus to draw near,
   and when he had he said to him:

"Dear friend, put out your hand,
my children, put yours here.
Now swear you never will abandon them
but wisely further all their needs
as friendship and the time will tell."
And Theseus, noble that he is, holding back his tears,
swore to keep his promise to his friend.

As soon as this was done,
Oedipus, groping for his daughters with blind hands,
said: "Sweet children, now be brave,
as you were born to be, and leave this place.
Do not ask to see what you should not see
or hear what you should not hear.
But go at once.
Only Theseus has the right to stay
and see what now unfolds."

Such was his converse. We heard it all of us.
So, sobbing with the girls, we left.
But after a little while, some paces off,
we glanced around
and Oedipus was nowhere to be seen
but only the King,
holding up his hands to screen his eyes
as if he had beheld a vision—
one too dazzling for a mortal's sight.
Then presently we saw him hail the earth and sky
in one great prayer.

[*The* MESSENGER *pauses*]

How Oedipus has passed, no man shall ever tell,
no man but Theseus.
For in that hour no whitehot thunderbolt from Zeus
came down,
no surge of giant sea to take him.
Some emissary maybe from heaven came;
or was the adamantine floor of the dead
gently reft for him with love?
The passing of the man was pangless
with no trace of pain nor any loud regret.

It was of mortal exits the most marvelous.
But if you think that none of this makes sense,
I am content to go on talking nonsense.

CHORUS

Where are the girls and their escort now?

MESSENGER

Not far away,
   for I hear the sound of sobbing.

[ANTIGONE *and* ISMENE, *escorted by a solemn company
of attendants, slowly walk into view*]

FOURTH CHORAL DIALOGUE

[*which lasts until the end of the play*]

Strophe I

ANTIGONE

Cry, cry, and cry again!
Our cause is too complete:
Two sisters and their sire
   Stained to the core.
Oh tears for the spellbound blood!
We lived his long-drawn life of pain
Until this dazing hour
   This last suffering
His ineffable demise.

CHORUS

What took place?

ANTIGONE

We can only guess.

CHORUS

So he is gone?

ANTIGONE

Gone as you would wish.
　No bloody war
No deep sea caught him up
　But he was plucked
By some unseen design:
Rapt to the land of blind horizons.
And now a deathlike night
Has blanketed our vision.
In distant lands, over drifting seas,
How shall we live our bitter living?

ISMENE

　I know not how.
Come blood-dripping Death
　And carry me down
And lay me by my ancient father's side.
　So should I miss
The unliveable life to come.

CHORUS

Dear children, stop your tears,
　You best of daughters.
Such is our end which heaven sends us
　And Fate is our friend.

Antistrophe I

ANTIGONE

Ah! What was pain was joy
What lacked all love was love

When I had him in my arms.
  Father, my father,
Wrapped in perpetual gloom
In that territory of shade—
Not even there shall her
  Love and mine
Be barred from you.

CHORUS

So his work is done?

ANTIGONE

He had his wish.

CHORUS

His wish?

ANTIGONE

He wished to die on foreign soil
  He did:
His bed beneath the mantle
  Of the gentle dark,
His aftermath of mourning
  Rich in tears.
  Oh Father, yes
I cannot staunch their flow,
It is a flood of sorrow . . .
To die on foreign soil,
You wanted that, but ah,
So far away from me!

ISMENE

  Poor dear sister,
With Father gone forever
What fate remains for you and me?

CHORUS

Dear children, think of this
He made a blessed end
   So cease your crying.
   There's none alive
   That's free from trial.

Strophe II

ANTIGONE

Dearest, let's go back there.

ISMENE

Whatever for?

ANTIGONE

I'm gripped with sudden longing.

ISMENE

What?

ANTIGONE

To see his hidden home.

ISMENE

Whose home?

ANTIGONE

Our father's.

ISMENE

It is forbidden. And also, don't you see . . .

ANTIGONE

Why this reluctance?

ISMENE

But don't you see . . .

ANTIGONE

I do not, go on.

ISMENE

He has no tomb.
He died away from all of us.

ANTIGONE

Then take me there and kill me too.

ISMENE

And leave me helpless and deserted,
    dragging out my hopeless life alone?

Antistrophe II

CHORUS

Bear up, dear girls, take heart!

ISMENE

But where, oh where
is there left to go?

CHORUS

There is a place . . .

ISMENE

But where?

CHORUS

Here. Nothing shall molest you here.

ISMENE

That I know.

CHORUS

Then what is on your mind?

ISMENE

We can't go home to Thebes.

CHORUS

Don't even try.

ISMENE

How terrible!

CHORUS

It always was.

ISMENE

No, worse
than the worst before.

CHORUS

I know, a surge of sorrow
sweeps over you.

ISMENE

Oh where are we to turn, great Zeus?
What hope, what destiny to drive us on,
    and what the use?

[*End of strophic pattern but not of Choral Dialogue.*
THESEUS *and his escort enter*]

THESEUS

Weep no more, sweet women.
Where death has dealt so kindly
There is no room for sorrow
or nemesis will follow.

ANTIGONE

Good son of Aegeus, we beg you . . .

THESEUS

Daughters, for what favor?

ANTIGONE

Let these eyes of ours regard
our father's place of resting.

THESEUS

That may not be.

ANTIGONE

But you are king of Athens. Why?

THESEUS

Because, dear children,
he himself has charged me
not to let a mortal being
approach these hallowed precincts
or invade with prayers and voices
his sanctuary of quiet.
And if I keep this covenant,
he said I keep my country
free from every hurt.
The gods' ears heard these pledges
And Zeus the god of treaties,
the all-seeing god, has sealed it.

ANTIGONE

Then if his wish be this,
enough for us. So be it.
But send us back to Thebes:
Thebes our ancestral city.
There we must try to stem
the bloodbath of our brothers.

THESEUS

Why, so I shall,
and spare no pains
to gladden you and grace his tomb:
the dauntless dead so lately swept away.

CHORUS

Come then cease your crying
Keep tears from overflowing
All's ordained past all denying.

ANTIGONE

for Clarissa

ΤΟ ΠΡΙΝ δομων ἀγαλμα

(to prin domōn aga(ma)

THE CHARACTERS

ANTIGONE, daughter of Oedipus and sister of Polyneices and Eteocles

ISMENE, sister of Antigone

CHORUS of Citizens of Thebes

CREON, king of Thebes and uncle of Antigone and Ismene

A SENTRY

HAEMON, son of Creon and betrothed to Antigone

TIRESIAS, a blind prophet

EURYDICE, wife of Creon and mother of Haemon

FIRST MESSENGER

Guards, Ladies-in-waiting, and a Boy

TIME AND SETTING

After the death of OEDIPUS, *his two sons contend for the throne of Thebes.* POLYNEICES, *leading the Seven Champions, attacks from Argos and batters at the seven gates of Thebes.* ETEOCLES *defends the city, supported by* CREON, *who appears to have been acting as regent. In a great battle the two brothers meet face to face and kill each other. The Argive forces retreat. It is the morning after the battle. The dead still lie on the field, including* POLYNEICES *and* ETEOCLES. CREON, *once again the undisputed master of Thebes, proclaims that* POLYNEICES, *because he died fighting against his own city, shall be left to rot on the battlefield—the most ignominious of ends for any Greek.* ANTIGONE, *caught in a conflict of loyalties, to her dead brother and to the State, decides to defy* CREON's *edict. It is daybreak. She calls her sister out from the palace.*

Antigone

ANTIGONE

Come, Ismene, my own dear sister, come!
What more do you think could Zeus require of us
  to load the curse that's on the House of Oedipus?
There is no sorrow left, no single shame,
  no pain, no tragedy,
  which does not hound us, you and me, towards our
                                                    end.

And now,
  what's this promulgation which they say
  our ruler has made to all the state?
Do you know? Have you heard?
Or are you sheltered from the news
  that deals a deathblow to our dearest?

ISMENE

Our dearest, Antigone? I've heard no news
  either good or bad,
  ever since we two were stripped
  of two brothers in a single day,
Each dismissing each by each other's hand.
And since the Argive army fled last night,
  I've heard no more—either glad or sad.

ANTIGONE

That's what I thought,
  that's why I've brought you here beyond the gates
  that you may hear my news alone.

ISMENE

What mischief are you hinting at?

ANTIGONE

I think you know . . . Our two dear brothers:
Creon is burying one to desecrate the other.
Eteocles, they say, he has dispatched with proper rites
    as one judged fit to pass in glory to the shades.
But Polyneices, killed as piteously,
    an interdict forbids that anyone should bury him
    or even mourn.
He must be left unwept, unsepulchered,
    a vulture's prize,
    sweetly scented from afar.
That's what they say our good and nobble Creon plans:
    plans for you and me, yes me;
And now he's coming here to publish it and make it
                             plain
    to those who haven't heard.
Anyone who disobeys will pay no trifling penalty
    but die by stoning
    before the city walls.
There's your chance to prove your worth,
    or else a sad degeneracy.

ISMENE

You firebrand! Could I do a thing
    to change the situation as it is?

ANTIGONE

You could. Are you willing
    to share danger and suffering and . . .

ISMENE

Danger? What are you scheming at?

ANTIGONE

. . . take this hand of mine to bury the dead?

ISMENE

What! Bury him and flout the interdict?

ANTIGONE

He is my brother still, and yours;
   though you would have it otherwise,
   but I shall not abandon him.

ISMENE

What! Challenge Creon to his face?

ANTIGONE

He has no right to keep me from my own.

ISMENE

Sister, please, please!
Remember how our father died:
   hated, in disgrace,
   self-dismantled in horror of himself,
   his own hand stabbing out his sight.
And how his mother-wife in one
   twisted off her earthly days with cord;
And thirdly how our two brothers in a single day
   each achieved for each a suicidal nemesis.
And now, we two are left.
Think how much worse our end will be than all the rest
   if we defy our sovereign's edict and his power.
Remind ourselves that we are women
   and as such are not made to fight with men.
For might unfortunately is right
   and makes us bow to things like this and worse.
Therefore shall I beg the shades below
   to judge me leniently as one who kneeled to force.
It's madness to meddle.

ANTIGONE

I will not press you any more.
I would not want you as a partner if you asked.
Go to what you please. I go to bury him.
How beautiful to die in such pursuit!
To rest loved by him whom I have loved,
    sinner of a holy sin,
With longer time to charm the dead than those who live,
    for I shall abide forever there.
So go. And please your fantasy
    and call it wicked what the gods call good.

ISMENE

You know I don't do that.
I'm just not made to war against the state.

ANTIGONE

Make your apologies!
I go to raise a tomb above my dearest brother.

ISMENE

You foolhardy thing! You frighten me.

ANTIGONE

Don't fear for me. Be anxious for yourself.

ISMENE

At least tell no one what you do, but keep it dark,
    and I shall keep it secret too.

ANTIGONE

Oh tell it, tell it, shout it out!
I'd hate your silence more than if you told the world.

ISMENE

So fiery—in a business that chills!

ANTIGONE

Perhaps, but I am doing what I must.

ISMENE

Yes, more than must. And you are doomed to fail.

ANTIGONE

Why then, I'll fail, but not give up before.

ISMENE

Don't plunge into such a hopeless enterprise.

ANTIGONE

Urge me so, and I shall hate you soon.
He, the dead, will justly hate you too.
Say that I'm mad, and madly let me risk
The worst that I can suffer and the best:
A death that martyrdom can render blest.

ISMENE

Go then, if you must toward your end:
Fool, wonderful fool, and loyal friend.

[ISMENE *watches* ANTIGONE *walk away, then she goes into the palace*]

ENTRY ODE

[*The* CHORUS *in a march-dance files into the theater, singing a hymn of triumph. They celebrate the defeat of the invading Polyneices and the victory of Thebes over Argos.*]

Strophe I

CHORUS

Sunshaft of the sun
Most resplendent sun
That ever shone on Thebes
The Seven Gates of Thebes:
Epiphany, you broke
Eye of the golden day
Marching over Dirce's streams
At dawn to drive in headlong flight
The warrior who came with shields
   All fulminant as snow
   In Argive stand at arms
Scattered now before the lancing sun.

LEADER

Propelled against our land
   By Polyneices's claims
This screaming eagle circled round
Caparisoned with arms he swooped
His wings their shields of snow. His crest
   Their helmets in the sun.

Antistrophe I

CHORUS

He stooped above our towers
Gaped above our gates
His hungry spears hovered
Then before he gorged
And glutted on our blood
Before Hephaestus hot
With pitch and flame had seized
Our crown of towers, all the din
That Ares loves burst around
   Their rear, and panic turned
   His flank. The fight came on
Behind their backs: a dragon-breathing foe.

LEADER

The braggart's pompous tongue
  Is hated most by Zeus
And seeing them advance superb
In clank of gold, he struck their first
Man down with fire before he yelled
  Triumph from the walls.

Strophe II

CHORUS

Thundering down to the ground with his torch
Knocked from his hands, this bacchanalian
Passionate lunatic breathing out hate
In hurricanes, fell in a flaming arc
His brandished torch all quenched, and great
Ares like a war horse wheeled:
Ubiquitous his prancing strength
  Trampling in the dust
Havoc that he dealt with several dooms.

LEADER

Seven champions dueled
  With seven at the Seven
Gates and gave their panoplies
To Zeus, save two, the fatal two
Who sharing parents shared their fall,
  Brother killing brother.

Antistrophe II

CHORUS

But now that this triumph, the loudest of triumphs,
Oh joy-bearing triumph! has come to our Thebes
The proud city of chariots, why
Now let us chase the memory far
Away of the wars that are blessedly past.
Come call on the gods with song and with dance

All through the night at the groves and the shrines,
  And Bacchus shall lead the round—
Shouting and shaking all Thebes with his revels.

LEADER

But look who comes, the lucky
  Son of Menoeceus:
The man the gods have made our king.
What new vicissitudes of state
Vex him now? Why has he sent
  A herald to our summons?

[CREON *has entered from the palace, surrounded by soldiers. He addresses the* CHORUS]

FIRST EPISODE

CREON

Gentlemen, the gods have graciously
  steadied our ship of state, which storms
  have terribly tossed.
And now I have called you here privately
  because of course I know
  your loyalty to the House of Laius.
How again, when Oedipus was king,
  your duty never faltered,
  and when he fell you still upheld his sons.
But now that they have gone,
  sharing their double end on a single day,
  (mutual murder, mutual recompense!),
I nearest in line enjoy the scepter and the throne.

Now, naturally, there is no way
  to tell the character and mettle of a man
  until you've seen him govern.
Nevertheless, I want to make it plain:
I am the kind of man who can't and never could
  abide the tongue-tied ruler who through fear
  backs away from sound advice.

And I find intolerable the man who puts his country
  second to his friends.
For instance, if I saw ruin and danger
  heading for the state,
  I would speak out.
Never could I make my country's enemy my private
                          friend,
  knowing as I do,
  she is the good ship that bears us safe.

So there you have my principles by which I govern.
In accord with them, I made the proclamation
  that you heard just now:
Eteocles, who died in arms for Thebes,
  shall have a glorious funeral
  as befits a hero going to join the noble dead.
But his brother Polyneices,
  he who came from exile breathing fire
  against this city of his fathers and its shrines;
The man who came all thirsting for his country's blood
  to drag the rest of us away as slaves—
I've sent the edict out
  that none shall bury him or even mourn.
He must be left all ghastly where he fell,
  a corpse for dogs to maul and vultures pick his bones.

You see the kind of man I am!
You'll not catch me putting traitors up on pedestals
  beside the loyal and true.
I'll honor him alone, alive or dead, who honors Thebes.

LEADER

Your disposition is quite clear,
  son of Menoeceus, Creon,
  touching friend or enemy of this our city.
We know you have the power too
  to wreak your will upon the living and the dead.

CREON

Then see to it my injunctions are performed.

LEADER

Put the burden on some younger men.

CREON

No. Sentries are already posted on the corpse.

LEADER

Then what exactly do you want us to do?

CREON

Merely see there're no infringements of the law.

LEADER

No man is mad enough to welcome death.

CREON

And death it is. But greed of gain
    has often made men fools.

[*A* SENTRY, *disheveled and distraught, comes bumbling
in towards the King*]

SENTRY

King, I won't pretend I come at breakneck speed,
    all out of breath.
I kept on stopping in my tracks . . . to think . . .
    and turning back.
I held committee meetings with myself:
"You fool," I said,
    "you're 'eading straight for the lion's mouth,"
    then, "Blockhead, what're you waiting for?
    if Creon gets the news from someone else, you're done!"

So I've come scurrying at a snail's pace
  by the long shortcut,
  the "forward" voice in charge.
And 'ere I am, with a tale to tell that makes no sense,
  which any'ow I'll tell, cos I do believe
  nothing bad can 'appen that isn't on one's ticket.

CREON

Come to the point, man! What are you dithering about?

SENTRY

First, sir, if I may slip in a word about miself.
It in't me that done it,
  and I dunno who darned done it neither;
  so it in't fair to make me take the rap.

CREON

Done it? Done it? You're a great marksman—
  hit the target first time!
You must have something very odd to say.

SENTRY

It's awfully off-putting, sir, to bring bad news—
  especially to you, sir.

CREON

Then get on with it and go.

SENTRY

Right! I'll tell you straight. The body—it's buried like.
I mean someone's just gorne and sprinkled dust on it—
  right proper thirsty dust—and gorne . . .
  done the ritual, sir, you see.

CREON

What are you saying, man? Who would have dared?

SENTRY

Don't ask me, sir!
There ain't no mark of pick or mattock,
  ground's all 'ard, unbroken,
  no wheel tracks neither:
  Not a sign of 'uman 'ands.
When the sentry of the morning watch pointed to it,
  there it was at dawn, the corpse,
  an ugly mystery that struck us dumb.
T'weren't exactly buried,
  just sprinkled with earth ritual like
  as if someone wanted to set it free.
No marks of dog or jackal neither—not a scratch.
Then we flew at one another, guard accusing guard.
It came near to blows.
There weren't no clue to clinch the quarrel.
Any one of us coulda done it. See!
No evidence to disprove any one of us—not a shred.
So we dared one another to pick up red-'ot iron,
  walk through fire, and swear by all the gods
He neither done the deed nor 'ad the slightest inkling
                                        who 'ad.
Well, one of us cut through the deadlock, saying . . .
(We went weak as straws when we 'eard it,
  cos there weren't no denying,
  nor coming out of it in one piece neither):
This fella there and then blurts out: "We gotta tell the
                                        King.
  There ain't no way to cover up."
He convinced the lot of us, so we drew straws.
And 'oo should be the unlucky one to win the prize
  but yours truly.
So 'ere I am, unwelcome *I* can tell, and un'appy too,
For there ain't no one likes the bringer of bad news.

LEADER

Sire, I've had misgivings from the first:
  could this be more than purely natural work?

CREON

Enough! You make me furious with such senile doddering remarks.
It's quite insufferable.
You really think they give a damn, the gods, about this
corpse?
Next you'll say they make it a priority to bury him in state,
and thank him for his burning down their altars,
sacking shrines, scouting laws, and raping all the land.
Or are the gods these days considerate to criminals?
Far from it! No, from the first,
there's been a group of grumblers in this town:
men who can hardly abide my rule,
who nod and whisper, chafing beneath my law,
who are not in love with it at all.
These are the ones, I'll warrant,
who have suborned my guards with bribes.
Ah, Money! Money is a currency that's rank.
Money topples cities to the ground,
seduces men away from happy homes,
corrupts the honest heart to shifty ways,
makes men crooked connoisseurs of vice.
But these plotters who have sold themselves,
every man jack of them,
Will end up, gentlemen,
with much more than he's bargained for.

[*He turns on the* SENTRY]

You there! Get this straight:
I swear by almighty Zeus whom I revere and serve,
that either you find the man who did this burial
and stand him here before my eyes,
or Hades itself will be too good for you
until you've first confessed to everything—
yes, hanging from a cross.
That perhaps will teach you, soldier,
where to look for profit
and that gold can glister from an evil source.
Ah! Money never makes as many as it mars.

SENTRY

Am I allowed a word, sir? Or do I just go?

CREON

Can't you see your very voice gets on my nerves?

SENTRY

'urts your ears, does it, sir? Or kinda your conscience?

CREON

What business of yours is it to diagnose my pain?

SENTRY

Because I only affect your ears; the culprit, your brain.

CREON

By God, what a born chatterer you are!

SENTRY

Maybe, but it weren't me that did the burying.

CREON

No, you just sold yourself for silver.

SENTRY

Oh, what a crying shame, when right reason reasons
                                          wrong!

CREON

A logic-chopper and a wit! But don't imagine *that*
    will save your skin.
If you fail to stand the man before my face,
    you'll find that dirty money pays in hurt.

[CREON *strides into the palace*]

SENTRY

Well, let's 'ope he's found. But caught or not
   (and only chance can tell), one thing's for sure:
   you won't catch me coming back again.
It's a goddam miracle I got out of 'ere alive.

[SENTRY *runs off*]

FIRST CHORAL ODE

[*The* CHORUS *of Citizens, in an intuitive foreshadowing
of both Creon's and Antigone's fate, contrast the prowess
and glory of human kind with the tragedy of their downfall when they overstep the mark. There is a veiled warning to Creon not to exceed humane bounds, but also, by
their listing all the predominantly masculine occupations
(sailing, plowing, hunting, fishing, domesticating animals,
verbal skills, building, making laws), they are advising
women like Antigone to beware of taking on what they
consider male roles.*]

Strophe I

Creation is a marvel and
Man its masterpiece. He scuds
Before the southern wind, between
The pounding white-piling swell.
He drives his thoroughbreds through Earth
(Great goddess inexhaustible)
And overturns her with the plow
Unfolding her from year to year.

Antistrophe I

The light-balanced light-headed birds
He snares; wild beasts of every kind.
In his nets the deep sea fish
Are caught. Oh, mastery of man!

The free forest animal
He herds; the roaming upland deer.
The shaggy horse he breaks to yoke
The unflagging mountain bull.

Strophe II

Training his agile thoughts
                volatile as air
He's civilized the world
                of words and wit and law.
With a roof against the sky,
                the javelin crystal frosts
The arrow-lancing rains,
                he's fertile in resource
Provident for all,
                healing all disease:
All but death, and death—
                death he never cures.

Antistrophe II

Beyond imagining wise:
                his cleverness and skills
Through labyrinthine ways
                for good and also ill.
Distinguished in his city
                when law-abiding, pious
But when he promulgates
                unsavory ambition,
Citiless and lost.
                And then I will not share
My hearth with him; I want
                no parcel of his thoughts.

SECOND EPISODE

[*The* SENTRY *returns, leading* ANTIGONE]

CHORUS

What visitation do I see from heaven?
And one I wish I could deny.
I am amazed. It is Antigone.
What! They bring you here in charge?
Poor Antigone, daughter of unlucky Oedipus.
Were you rash enough to cross the King?
And did they take you in your folly?

SENTRY

'ere she is, the culprit: caught red'anded
    in the very act of burying 'im.
But where is Creon?

CHORUS

Coming from the house, and just in time.

[*Enter* CREON]

CREON

Just in time for what?

SENTRY

King, it's most unwise, I find,
    ever to promise not to do a thing.
Now look at me! I could 'ave sworn
    I'd not come scurrying back,
After being almost skinned alive by all your flailing
                                                threats.
Yet 'ere I am against my oath, bringing in this girl,
    and all because beyond my wildest dreams,
    in fact with quite a thrill,
    I caught 'er at it—actually at the burying.

No drawing straws this time—I'll say not!
So grab 'er, King, she's yours.
And I'm scot-free, or I should 'ope,
 quit of this 'ole goddam thing.

CREON

Tell me first when and how you found her.

SENTRY

She was burying the man. There ain't nothing more to tell.

CREON

Are you rambling? Do you know what you are saying?

SENTRY

Sir, I saw 'er in the act
 of burying that forbidden corpse.
Is that plain and clear?

CREON

But how actually was she surprised and taken?

SENTRY

Well it was like this.
We 'ad returned to the spot,
 our ears ringing with all your nasty threats,
 and 'ad brushed the earth from off the body
 to make it bare again
 (it was all soft and clammy),
And were squatting there windward of the stench,
 keeping each other up to the mark
And rounding 'ard on anybody that nodded . . .
Watching we were, till the midday sun,
 a great blazing ball
 bashed down on us something fierce,

When suddenly came this right twisting squall,
  sweeping across the plain,
  tearing the leaves off trees,
  buffeting 'eaven itself.
We 'ad to shut our eyes against this god-sent blight.
When at last it cleared
  there was this vision of this girl,
Standing there she was,
  giving out little shrill-like sobs:
  'eartrending as a mother bird's
  what 'as seen its nest pillaged
  and its bairns all gone.
That's 'ow she was wailing
  and calling curses down
  on them what done it
  when she saw the body bared.
Immediately she scoops up earth—a dry 'andful like—
  and sprinkles it. Then 'olding up
  a shapely brazen urn, she pours
  three libations for the dead.
That's when we swooped and closed upon our quarry.
She didn't flinch, and when we charged 'er
  with what she'd gorne and done,
  and done before, she just admitted it.
It made me glad and sad:
  bliss to get myself out of trouble,
  distress to bring it on a friend.
When all's said and done, 'owever,
  the safety of one's own sweet skin comes first.

CREON

Come girl, you with downcast eyes,
  did you, or did you not, do this deed?

ANTIGONE

I did. I deny not a thing.

CREON

You, soldier, you can go—be off wherever you please—
Free of any serious charge.

[*The* SENTRY *stands for a moment, smiles, then bounds
away*]

Now tell me, Antigone, a straight yes or no:
Did you know an edict had forbidden this?

ANTIGONE

Of course I knew. Was it not publicly proclaimed?

CREON

So you chose flagrantly to disobey my law?

ANTIGONE

Naturally! Since Zeus never promulgated such a law,
Nor will you find that Justice,
   Mistress of the world below,
   publishes such laws to humankind.
I never thought your mortal edicts had such force
   they nullified the laws of heaven,
   which unwritten, not proclaimed,
   can boast a currency that everlastingly is valid,
   an origin beyond the birth of man.
And I, whom no man's frown can frighten,
Am far from risking heaven's frown by flouting these.
I need no trumpeter from you to tell me I must die,
   we all die anyway
And if this hurries me to death before my time,
   why, such a death is gain. Yes, surely gain
   to one whom life so overwhelms.
Therefore, I can go to meet my end
   without a trace of pain.
But had I left the body of my mother's son unburied,
   lying where he lay,
   ah, that would hurt!
For this, I feel no twinges of regret.

And if you judge me fool, perhaps it is
    because a fool is judge.

LEADER

My word! The daughter is as headstrong as the father.
Submission is a thing she's never learned.

CREON

You wait and see! The toughest will
    is first to break: like hard untempered steel
    which snaps and shivers at a touch
    when hot from off the forge.
And I have seen high-mettled horses curbed
    by a little scrap of bit.
One who has no more authority than a common slave
    can ill afford to put on airs.
And yet, this girl, already versed in disrespect
    the first time she disobeyed my law,
Now adds a second insult, has done it again,
    and vaunts it to my face.
Oh, she's the man, not I,
    if she can flout authority and walk away unscathed.
I swear I hardly care
    if she be my sister's child
    or linked to me by blood more closely
    than any member of my hearth and home;
She and her sister will not now escape
    the utmost penalty.
I say the sister too.
I charge her as accomplice of this burial.
Call her forth.
I saw her whimpering in there just now, all gone to
                         pieces.

So does remorse blurt out the secret sin . . .
Although its opposite is even worse:
    crime detected glorifying crime.

ANTIGONE

Is there something more you want? Or just my life?

CREON

Not a thing, by God! It gives me what I want.

ANTIGONE

Why dawdle, then? Your conversation
  is hardly something I enjoy, or ever could,
  nor mine be more acceptable to you.
And yet it ought to be.
Where could I win respect and praise more validly than
                             this:
  burial of my brother?
Not a man here would say the opposite,
  were his tongue not locked in fear.
Unfortunately, tyranny (blessed in so much else besides)
  can lay the law down any way it wants.

CREON

Your view is hardly shared by all these Thebans here.

ANTIGONE

They think as I, but trim their tongues to you.

CREON

Are you not ashamed to differ from such men?

ANTIGONE

There is no shame to reverence relatives.

CREON

And the other duelist who died—was he no relative?

ANTIGONE

He was. And of the same father and same mother.

CREON

So, slighting one, you would salute the other?

ANTIGONE

The dead man would not agree with you on this.

CREON

Surely! If you make the hero honored with the black-
guard.

ANTIGONE

It was his brother not his slave that died.

CREON

Yes, ravaging our land, while *he* fell as its champion.

ANTIGONE

Hades makes no distinction in its rites and honors.

CREON

The just and unjust do not urge an equal claim.

ANTIGONE

The "crime" (who knows?) may be called a virtue there.

CREON

Not even death can metamorphose hate to love.

ANTIGONE

No, nor decompose my love to hate.

CREON

Curse you! Find the outlet for your love down there.
No woman while I live shall govern me.

[ISMENE *is brought in under guard*]

LEADER OF CHORUS

See where Ismene comes
Crying from the palace gates,
Her face all flushed.
A sister's tears are breaking rains
Upon her cheeks and from her eyes,
Her loveliness a shadow.

CREON

[*Turning viciously towards* ISMENE]

Come, you serpent, secret lurker in my home,
　who sucked my blood
Even while I nurtured you two sister vipers at my
　　　　　　　　　　　　　　　　　　　　throne—
Speak. Confess your part in burying him.
Or do you dare deny complicity?

ISMENE

I did it too. If she'll allow my claim.
I share with her the credit and the blame.

ANTIGONE

That is not true. You do not share with me,
　nor did I grant you partnership.

ISMENE

But now that your poor ship is buffeted,
　I'm not ashamed to sail the voyage at your side.

ANTIGONE

The dead of Hades know whose act it was.
I do not take to those who take to talk.

ISMENE

Sister, do not scorn me; let me share
   your death and holy homage to the dead.

ANTIGONE

No share in work, no share in death,
   and I must consummate alone what I began.

ISMENE

Then what is left of life to me when you are gone?

ANTIGONE

Ask Creon. You and he are friends.

ISMENE

Ah! Must you jeer at me? It does not help.

ANTIGONE

You are right. It is a joyless jeering.

ISMENE

Tell me, even now: how can I help?

ANTIGONE

Save yourself. I shall not envy you.

ISMENE

Poor dear sister—let me suffer with you!

ANTIGONE

No. For you choose life, and I chose death.

ISMENE

When all my protests were of no avail.

ANTIGONE

We played our different parts, with different acclaim.

ISMENE

But now we share and equal share of blame.

ANTIGONE

Look up! You live! And I died long ago,
    when I gave my life to serve the dead.

CREON

These girls, I swear, are crazed: one mad by birth,
    the other by attainment.

ISMENE

Yes, my lord, for when misfortune comes,
    he sends our reason packing out of doors.

CREON

And yours went flying fast
    when you chose damnation with the damned.

ISMENE

Yet, with her gone, what portion had I left?

CREON

Do not mention *her*. She does not still exist.

ISMENE

You would not kill your own son's bride?

CREON

Let him sow his seed in other furrows.

ISMENE

A match like theirs will *not* repeat itself.

CREON

I shudder at the jades who court our sons.

ANTIGONE

My darling Haemon, how your father heaps disgrace on you!

CREON

Damn you and damn your cursed marriage!

LEADER

You would not tear your own son's bride from him?

CREON

Let us say that Death is going to come between.

LEADER

I fear, I fear it's fixed. Her death is sealed.

CREON

Yes, let us both be quite assured of *that*.
Guards, take them away and lock them up.
No more roaming. They are women now.
The breath of Hades pressing close to kill
Can make the bravest turn, and turn the bravest will.

[ANTIGONE *and* ISMENE *are led away.* CREON *stays*]

SECOND CHORAL ODE

[*The* CHORUS *cries out in an ode which begins by being both a lament for the past victimization of the House of Oedipus and an omen for the present, and then goes on to warn all those who think they can live their lives apart from the universal providence of Zeus.*]

Strophe I

Happy the man who has not sipped the bitter day,
Whose house is firm against divine assault.
   No planted curse creeps on and on
Through generations like the dark and driven surge
Booming from the bosom of the sea while Thracian gales
Churn perpetually the ooze in waves that throw
Down upon the headlands swept and carded by the storm
   Their thunderous mass.

Antistrophe I

So do I see the house of Labdacus struck down,
In all its generations victimized by some
   Pursuing deity. Its useless dead.
Its never-ending doom. And now once more the sun
Gone down in blood: the final hope of Oedipus
Felled to the root, put out in smoke and Hades' dust,
And all because of headlong folly and the reckless speech
   Of a frenzied heart.

Strophe II

O Zeus, what creature pits himself against thy power?
Not Sleep encumbrous with his sublet net
   And not the menstrual cycle
      Of the tireless moon.
Thou in ancient splendors still art young
      When worlds are old
      On Mount Olympus.
   Everything past, everything present,

And everything still to come
Is thy domain
No mortal thing however vast can steal
Outside thy grasp.

Antistrophe II

Hope, eternally gadding, alights on many with nothing
But bliss, but just as blithely brings to others
Delusions and seething ambition.
No man can tell
What has come stealthily creeping over his life
Until too late
Hot ashes and pain
Sear his feet . . . Once long ago
A sage famously said:
"If evil good appear
To any, the gods are near. Unscathed he'll go,
And then they'll bring him low."

[HAEMON *is seen approaching*]

LEADER

Here Haemon comes, your youngest son,
Driven perhaps by pangs of grief
For Antigone his sentenced bride:
A bitter groom, a marriage marred.

CREON

We shall see in a moment, and without the need of seers.

THIRD EPISODE

[HAEMON *enters. The men stare warily at each other for a few seconds*]

CREON

Son, do you come provoked against your father
for the death warrant of your would-be bride,
or still my loving son, whatever I may do?

HAEMON

Father, I am your loving son and you the wise
    preceptor of my ways, whom I must follow.
No marriage I could make would ever match
    the good of your abiding counsel.

CREON

Well spoken son!
Just what a right-minded son should feel:
    unremitting deference to his father's will.
Such is a parent's prayer, to see grow up
    a race of filial sons to deck his home:
Ready always to avenge their father's wrongs,
    and of course to give his friends
    the selfsame honor that the father gives.
But a man who raises a batch of worthless boys,
    what has he hatched for himself but nuisances,
    and jubilant sneers from the ill-disposed!

Oh Haemon, don't lose your balance for a woman's sake!
Don't hug a joy that's cheap and cools:
    an evil woman for your bed and board.
No wound is worse than counterfeited love.
She is poison. Spit her out.
Let her go and find a mate in Hades.
Why, I've just caught her in an open act of treason—
    she alone of all the city.
I *will* not break my word to Thebes. She dies.
So let her plead to Zeus
    the sanctity of kindred ties.

How can I, if I nurse sedition in my house,
   not foster it outside?
No. If a man can keep his home in hand,
   he proves his competence to keep the state.
But one who breaks the law and flouts authority,
   I never will allow.
Unswerving submission
   to whomsoever the state has put in charge
   is what is asked: in little things as well as great,
   in right and wrong.
And I am confident that one who thus obeys,
   will make a perfect subject or a perfect king:
   the kind of man who in the thick of flying spears
   never flinches from his post
   but stands dauntless at his comrade's side.
But as for anarchy,
   there is no greater curse than anarchy.
It topples cities down, it crumbles homes,
   it shatters allied ranks in broken flight
   which discipline kept whole:
For discipline preserves and orders well.
Let us then defend authority
   and not be ousted by a girl.
If yield we must, then let it be to men,
And never have it said we were worsted by a woman.

LEADER

What you say (unless my wits have run to seed)
   sounds reasonable and makes good sense.

HAEMON

Yes, Father, reason: the gods' greatest gift to man.
   I would not dream of criticizing yours
   or saying you were wrong, even if I could.
But other men can reason rightly too.

As your son, you see, I find myself
   marking every word and act and comment of the crowd,
   to gauge the temper of the simple citizen,
   who dares not risk your scowl to speak his mind.
But I from the shadows hear them:
   hear a city's sympathy for this girl,
   because no woman ever faced
   so unreasonable, so cruel a death,
   for such a generous cause.
She would not leave her brother where he fell,
   for carrion birds and dogs to maul.
"Should not her name be writ in gold?" they say,
   and so the whisper grows.

You know, my Father, how I prize
   your well-being and your name.
For sons and father's crown each other's glory
   with each other's fame.
So I beg you Father,
   don't entrench yourself in your opinion
   as if everyone else was wrong.
The kind of man who always thinks that he is right,
   that his opinions, his pronouncements,
   are the final word,
   is usually exposed as hollow as they come.
But a wise man is flexible, has much to learn
   without a loss of dignity.
See the trees in floodtime, how they bend
   along the torrent's course,
   and how their twigs and branches do not snap,
   but stubborn trees are torn up roots and all.
In sailing too, when fresh weather blows,
   a skipper who will not slaken sail, turns turtle,
   finishes his voyage beam-ends up.

So let your anger cool, and change your mind.
I may be young but not without some sense.
Let men be wise by instinct if they can,
   but when this fails and nature won't oblige,
   be wise by good advice.

LEADER

Sire, the young man speaks good sense: worth listening to.
And you, son, too, should listen. You both speak to the
point.

CREON

You mean that men of my years have to learn to think
 by taking notes from men of his?

HAEMON

In only what is right.
 It is my merit not my years that count.

CREON

Your merit is to foment lawlessness.

HAEMON

You know I do not plead for criminals.

CREON

So this creature is no criminal, eh?

HAEMON

The whole of Thebes says "no."

CREON

And I must let the mob dictate my policy?

HAEMON

See now who is speaking like a boy!

CREON

Do *I* rule this state, or someone else?

HAEMON

A one man state is no state at all.

CREON

The state is his who rules it. Is that plain?

HAEMON

The state that you should rule would be a desert.

CREON

This boy is hopelessly on the woman's side.

HAEMON

I'm on your side. Are you a woman then?

CREON

You reprobate! At open loggerheads with your father!

HAEMON

On the contrary: you at loggerheads with open justice!

CREON

My crime, of course, the discharge of my rule.

HAEMON

What rule—when you trample on the rule of heaven?

CREON

Insolent pup! A woman's lackey!

HAEMON

Lackey to nothing of which I am ashamed.

CREON

Not ashamed to be the mouthpiece for that trollop?

HAEMON

I speak for you, for me, and for the holy spirits of the dead.

CREON

The dead? Precisely—you'll never marry her alive.

HAEMON

Well then, dead—one death beckoning to another.

CREON

So it's come to that—you threaten me?

HAEMON

One cannot threaten empty air!

CREON

My word, what wisdom! How you'll regret dispensing it!

HAEMON

If you weren't my father, I'd say your mind had gone.

CREON

You woman's slave! Don't come toadying to me!

HAEMON

Go on—make remarks and never listen to an answer!

CREON

Is that so? Then by Olympus be quite sure of this:
You shall not rant and jeer at me without reprisal.
Off with the wretched girl! I say she dies
In front of him, before her bridegroom's eyes.

HAEMON

She shall not die—don't think it—
   in my sight or by my side.
And you shall never see my face again.
I commit you raving to your chosen friends.

[HAEMON *rushes out*]

LEADER

Gone, your Majesty, but gone distraught.
He is young, his rage will make him desperate.

CREON

Let him do or dream up acts as murderous as a fiend's,
   these girls, he shall not snatch from death.

LEADER

You do not mean to kill them both?

CREON

You are right. Not the one who did not meddle.

LEADER

What kind of death do you plan?

CREON

I'll take her down a path untrod by man.
I'll hide her living in a rock-hewn vault,
With ritual food enough to clear the taint
Of murder from the City's name.
I'll leave her pleading to her favorite god,
Hades. He may charm her out a way to life.
Or perhaps she'll learn though late the cost
Of homage to the dead is labor lost.

[CREON *walks away into the palace*]

THIRD CHORAL ODE

[*The* CHORUS, *apprehensive of the fate of the young lovers, sings of the desperately destructive power of love. Their words also veil a condemnation of men like* CREON, *who overvalue the so-called masculine qualities of the soul and fail to realize the duality of male and female within the person.*]

Strophe I

Love, unquelled in battle
Love, making nonsense of wealth
Pillowed all night on the cheek of a girl
You roam the seas, pervade the wilds
And in a shepherd's hut you lie.
Shadowing immortal gods
You dog ephemeral man—
Madness your possession.

Antistrophe I

Turning the wise into fools
You twist them off their course
And now you have stung us to this strife
Of father fighting son . . . Oh, Love,
The bride has but to glance
With the lyrical light of her eyes
To win you a seat in the stars
And Aphrodite laughs.

[*End of Choral Ode and beginning of Choral Dialogue which continues through* FOURTH EPISODE]

FOURTH EPISODE

[ANTIGONE *is led in under guard*]

LEADER

And now you turn on me
Unman my loyalty
Loose my tears to see
You Antigone
Pass your wedding bower
Death's chamber, pass
So easily.

Strophe I

[ANTIGONE *and the* CHORUS *chant alternately*]

ANTIGONE

See me, friends and citizens,
Look on this last walk—
The sun's light snuffed out with my dower
And Death leading me to Acheron
Alive, where all must sleep.
No wedding march, no bridal song
Cheer me on my way,
I whom Hades Lord of the dark lake weds.

CHORUS

Yet you walk with fame, bedecked
In praise towards the dead man's cave.
No sickness severed you
No sword incited struck.
All mistress of your fate you move
Alive, unique, to Hades Halls.

Antistrophe I

ANTIGONE

Oh, but I have heard what happened
To that Phrygian girl, poor foreigner
(The child of Tantalus), who clings
Like ivy on the heights of Sipylus
Captured in stone, petrified
Where all the rains, they say, the flying snow,
Waste her form away which weeps
In waterfalls. I feel her trance,
Her lonely exodus, in mine.

CHORUS

And she a goddess born of gods
While we are mortals born of men.
What greater glory for a woman's end
To partner gods in death
Who partnered them in life!

Strophe II

ANTIGONE

Ah! Now you laugh at me.
Thebes, Thebes, by all our father's gods
You my own proud chariot city
Can you not wait till I am gone?
And you sweet Dirce's stream and Theban groves
You at least be witnesses to me with love
Who walk in dismal passage to my heavy tomb
Unwept, unjustly judged
Displaced from every home
Disowned by both the living and the dead.

Strophe III

CHORUS

Perhaps you aimed too high
You dashed your foot on Fate
Where Justice sits enthroned.
You fall a plummet fall
To pay a father's sin.

Antistrophe II

ANTIGONE

You touch my wounds, my memories
Make fresh again my tears: the triple curse
That haunts the House of Labdacus:
The spilt and tainted blood, the horrid bed,
My fated mother sleeping with her son
To father me in incest . . . Parents here I come,
Home at last, not wed, no broken spell.
Brother when you made
Your blindfold match, you made
Your death and mine—mine to come.

Antistrophe III

CHORUS

Pious is as pious does
But where might is right
It's reckless to do wrong.
Self-propelled to death
You go with open eyes.

Epode

ANTIGONE

Unwept, unwedded, unloved I go
On this last journey of all.
Eye of the blessed sun—

I shall miss you soon.
No tears will mourn me dead.
No friend to cry.

[*End of Choral Dialogue.* CREON *has entered*]

CREON

Listen you!
Panegyrics and dirges go on forever
    if given the chance.
Dispatch her at once, I say. Seal up the tomb.
Let her choose a death at leisure—or perhaps,
    in her new home,
An underground life forlorn.
We wash our hands of this girl—
    except to take her from the light.

ANTIGONE

Come tomb, my wedding chamber, come!
You sealed off habitations of the grave!
My many family dead, finished, fetched
    in final muster to Persephone.
I am last to come, and lost the most of all,
    my life still in my hands.
And yet I come (I hope I come) toward a father's love,
    beloved by my mother,
And by you, my darling brother, loved.
Yes, all of you,
Whom these my hands have washed, prepared and sped
    with ritual to your burials.
And now, sweet Polyneices, dressing you,
    I've earned this recompense,
    though richly honored you the just will say.

No husband dead and gone, no children lisping "mother"
    ever could have forced me to withstand
    the city to its face.
By what law do I assert so much? Just this:

A husband dead, another can be found,
  a child replaced, but once a brother's lost
  (mother and father dead and buried too)
No other brother can be born or grows again.
That is my principle,
  which Creon stigmatized as criminal,
  my principle for honoring you, my dearest brother.

So taken, so am I led away:
  a virgin still, no nuptial song, no marriage-bed,
  no children to my name.
An outcast stripped of sympathy,
  I go alive toward these sepulchers of death.
What ordinance, what law of heaven broken,
  what god left for me to cast my eyes toward,
  when sacraments must now be damned as sacrilege?
And if these things be smiled upon by heaven,
  why, when I'm dead I'll know I sinned.
But if I find the sin was theirs,
  may Justice then mete out no less to them
  than what injustice now metes out to me—my doom.

LEADER

See how she goes, headlong driven
By the capricious gusts of her own will!

CREON

Putting to disgrace her loitering guards.
Who shall be paid their just rewards.

ANTIGONE

Ah, Death comes nearer with those words!

CREON

There is no comfort I can offer
Nor this damnation can I alter.

ANTIGONE

See me, Thebes, I am going, now going!
See me, divine ancestral Thebes!
Cast but a glance, you her princes,
On this last and lonely royal scion,
See what I suffer from these men
For reverencing the rights of man.

[ANTIGONE *is led away*]

FOURTH CHORAL ODE

[*The* CHORUS, *in an attempt to comfort* ANTIGONE, *recall situations of fate similar to her own. First there was Danäe, shut up by her father in a brazen tower because an oracle had foretold that she would bear a son who would kill him. Zeus, however, had access to her prison and impregnated her in a shower of gold. The resulting offspring, Perseus, did indeed later kill his grandfather (accidentally). Next, there was Lycurgus, son of Dryas king of Thrace: punished by Dionysus for insulting him and abolishing the cult of the vine in his kingdom. Lastly, there was Phineus, who, suspicious of his two sons by his first wife (daughter of Boreas, the north wind), prompted his second wife to blind them in a fit of jealousy.**]

Strophe I

Hidden from the sun
Housed behind brass doors
Danäe's beauty too was locked away
Her nuptial cell a tomb
And she, my child, yes she
A royal daughter too:

---

*It must be borne in mind that there are contradictory versions of these stories in Greek mythology. Here, for instance, Sophocles's account scrambles or conflates several others.

The rare receptacle of Zeus's golden seed.
O Destiny, marked mysterious force!
No mound of coins
No panoplies of war
No ramparts keep you out
And through the dark sea looming
    No ship escapes.

Antistrophe I

The savage son of Dryas
That Edonian king
Was pent by Dionysus in a prison
Clamped within a rocky cavern.
There his jeering changing
Changing into howling
Faded into echoes till he came at last
To know the godhead whom his madness
Baited when he tried
To quench the god-possessed
Flaring Bacchantes
And offended all the Muses
    Who love the flute.

Strophe II

Once in primitive Thrace near Salmydessus
Where twin black doom-ridden crags
Sever two seas, along the vicious
Lonely shores of the Bosporus,
War-loving Ares
Witnessed a nightmare scene:
The bride of Phineus, jealous, frenzied,
Plunging the dagger of her spindle
Into the princely eyes of his two sons . . .
Saw their vacant scream for vengeance
Plead in pools of socket-bloody staring.

Antistrophe II

Wasting in agony, doomed so cruelly
They lamented their mother's fatal mating
From which even her noble birthline
From Erechtheus could not save her—
And she a daughter cradled
By Boreas in the caverns
Born amid her father's tempests
Bolting like a colt from heaven
Over the uplands—child of the gods—

Even she, Antigone, they had her,
The ageless gray-grim Fates they struck her down.

FIFTH EPISODE

[*The blind prophet* TIRESIAS, *led by a boy, announces his arrival in a quavering, chanting voice*]

TIRESIAS

Rulers of Thebes, here we come: one pair of eyes for
                                                two
On a single road, and the blind man led by another.

CREON

What news, venerable Tiresias?

TIRESIAS

I shall tell you, and you must listen hard.

CREON

Have I ever failed to listen to you?

TIRESIAS

And therefore have you safely piloted the state.

CREON

Gladly do I own my debt to you.

TIRESIAS

Then beware, you're standing once again upon the
                                    razor's edge.

CREON

How so? Your words and aspect chill.

TIRESIAS

Listen, I'll read the signs and make them plain.
I was sitting by my ancient chair of augury,
    the haunt of every kind of bird,
When suddenly a noise not heard before
    assaults my ears:
A panic screeching and a pandemonium deafening jargon:
    beaks and bloody talons tearing—I could tell it—
    pinions whirring,
    all shocked me as a portent.
At once I kindled sacrifice to read by fire,
    but Hephaestus fanned no leaping flame.
Instead, a sort of sweat distilled from off the thigh fat,
    slid in smoke upon the sputtering fire.
The gallbladders burst and spurted up.
The grease oozed down and left the thighbones bare.
These were the signs I learnt from off this boy,
    omens of a ruined sacrifice:
    he is my eyes as I am yours.

See it—how the city sickens, Creon,
    these the symptoms, yours the fanatic will that caused
                                    them:

Dogs and crows all glutted carrying
   desecrated carrion to the hearths and altars—
   carrion from the poor unburied son of Oedipus.
Burnt offerings go up in stench. The gods are dumb.
The birds of omen cannot sing.
But obscene vultures flap away
   with crops all gorged on human flesh.

Think, son, think! To err is human, true,
   and only he is damned who having sinned
      will not repent, will not repair.
He is a fool, a proved and stubborn fool.
Give death his due, and do not kick a corpse.
Where is renown to kill a dead man twice?
Believe me, I advise you well.
It should be easy to accept advice
   so sweetly tuned to your good use.

CREON

Old man,
   you pot away at me like all the rest
   as if I were a bull's-eye,
And now you aim your seer craft at me.
Well, I'm sick of being bought and sold
   by all your soothsaying tribe.
Bargain away! All the silver of Sardis,
   all the gold of India
   is not enough to buy this man a grave;
Not even if Zeus's eagles come, and fly away
   with carrion morsels to their master's throne.
Even such a threat of such a taint
   will not win this body burial.
It takes much more than human remains
   to desecrate the majesty divine.
Old man Tiresias,
The most reverend fall from grace when lies are sold
Wrapped up in honeyed words—and all for gold.

TIRESIAS

Creon! Creon!
Is no one left who takes to heart that . . .

CREON

Come, let's have the platitude!

TIRESIAS

. . . That prudence is the best of all our wealth.

CREON

As folly is the worst of all our woes?

TIRESIAS

Yes, infectious folly! And you are sick with it.

CREON

I'll not exchange a fish-wife's set-to with a seer.

TIRESIAS

Which is what you do when you say I sell my prophecies.

CREON

As prophets do—a money-grubbing race.

TIRESIAS

Or as kings, who grub for money in the dung.

CREON

You realize this is treason—lese majesty?

TIRESIAS

Majesty? Yes, thanks to me you are savior of Thebes.

CREON

And you are not without your conjuring tricks. But still
a crook.

TIRESIAS

Go on! You will drive me to divulge something that . . .

CREON

Out with it! But not for money, please.

TIRESIAS

Unhappily for you this can't be bought.

CREON

Then don't expect to bargain with my wits.

TIRESIAS

All right then! Take it if you can.
A corpse for a corpse the price, and flesh for flesh,
  one of your own begotten.
The sun shall not run his course for many days
  before you pay.
You plunged a child of light into the dark;
  entombed the living with the dead; the dead
Dismissed unmourned, denied a grave—a corpse
Unhallowed and defeated of his destiny below.
Where neither you nor gods must meddle,
  you have thrust your thumbs.
Do not be surprised that heaven—yes, and hell—
  have set the Furies loose to lie in wait for you,
 Ready with the punishments you engineered for others.

Does this sound like flattery for sale?
Yet a little while and you shall wake
  to wailing and gnashing of teeth in the house of Creon.

Lashed to a unison of rage, they'll rise,
  those other cities,
  whose mangled sons received their obsequies
  from dogs and prowling jackals—
  from some filthy vulture flapping to alight
  before their very hearths to bring them home—
  desecration reeking from its beak.

There! You asked, and I have shot my angry arrows.
I aimed at your intemperate heart. I did not miss.
Come, boy, take me home.
Let him spew his choler over younger men.
He'll learn a little modesty in time,
  a little meekness soon.

[TIRESIAS *is led out by his boy.* CREON *stands motionless,
visibly shaken*]

LEADER

There's fire and slaughter for you, King!
The man has gone,
  but my gray hairs were long since shining black
  before he ever stirred the city to a false alarm.

CREON

I know. You point the horns of my dilemma.
It's hard to eat my words, but harder still
  to court catastrophe through overriding pride.

LEADER

Son of Menoeceus, be advised in time.

CREON

To do what? Tell me, I shall listen.

LEADER

Go free the maiden from her vault.

Then entomb the lonely body lying stark.

CREON

You really mean it—that I must yield?

LEADER

Must, King, and quickly too.
The gods, provoked, never wait to mow men down.

CREON

How it goes against the grain
  to smother all one's heart's desire!
But I cannot fight with destiny.

CHORUS

Quickly, go and do it. Don't trust to others.

CREON

Yes, I go at once.
Servants, servants—on the double!
You there, fetch the rest. Bring axes all
  and hurry to the hill.
My mind's made up. I'll not be slow
  to let her loose myself
  who locked her in the tomb.
In the end it is the ancient codes—oh my regrets!—
  that one must keep:
To value life then one must value law.

[CREON *and servants hurry away in all directions*]

FIFTH CHORAL ODE

[*The* CHORUS *sings a desperate hymn to Bacchus, begging him to come and save the city of Thebes and the stricken House of Oedipus*]

Strophe I

Calling you by a hundred names
Jewel and flower of Semele's wedding
Son of Zeus and son of thunder
Singer of sweet Italy!
Calling you in world communion
In the bowery lap of Dio's glades
Close by Ismenus's quicksilver stream:
You the Bacchus haunting Thebes
(Mother of the Bacchanals)
Hard by the very fields where once
    The dragon's teeth were sown.

Antistrophe I

Bacchus and your nymphs Bacchantes
Dancing in the hills and valleys:
Dots of fire and wreathing torches
Curling smoke above the crested
Forks (Castalia fled Apollo
Plunging into the spring-fed pool there)
Calling you from the slopes of Nyssa
Dripping ivy down to the seashore
Green with vineyards, while your Maenads
Storm ecstatic shouting "Bacchus"
    On your march to Thebes.

Strophe II

Calling you to your favorite city
Sacred city of your mother
(Ravished by a lightning bolt)
Calling you to a city dying—
People shadowed by the plague
Calling you to leave the high-spots
Leaping fleet-foot down to cross
The moaning waters. Oh come quickly
    Hurry from Parnassus.

Antistrophe II

Come you master of the dancing
Fiery-breathing pulsing stars
Steward of the midnight voices
Son of Zeus, O Prince appear!
Bring your train of Maenads raving
Swirling round you, round you dancing
Through the night, and shouting "Bacchus
Giver of all blessings, Bacchus!"
    Bacchus, oh come!

[*There is a pause, while the strains of the* CHORUS *die away. A* MESSENGER *enters*]

EPILOGUE

MESSENGER

Men of the House of Cadmus and of Amphion,
  how rash it is to envy others or despair!
The luck we adulate in one today,
  tomorrow is another's tragedy.
There is no stable horoscope for man.
Take Creon:
  he if anyone, I thought was enviable.
He saved this land from all our enemies,
  attained the pomp and circumstance of king,
  his children decked like olive branches round his
                              throne.
And now it is undone, all finished.
And what is left is not called life but death alive.
His kingly state is nothing to him now
  with gladness gone:
Vanity of vanities—the shadow of a shade.

LEADER

What fresh news do you bring of royal ruin?

MESSENGER

Death twice over, and the living guilty for the dead.

LEADER

Who struck and who is stricken? Say.

MESSENGER

Haemon's gone. Blood spilt by his own hand.

LEADER

By his own hand? Or by his father's?

MESSENGER

Both. Driven to it by his father's murdering.

LEADER

Oh Prophet, your prophecy's come true!

MESSENGER

So stands the case. Make of it what you will.

LEADER

Look, I see Eurydice approach,
    Creon's unhappy queen.
Is it chance or has she heard the deathknell of her son?

[EURYDICE *staggers in, supported by her maids*]

EURYDICE

Yes, good citizens, all of you, I heard:
Even as I went to supplicate
    the goddess Pallas with my prayers.

Just as I unloosed the bolt that locks the door,
   the sound of wailing struck my ears,
   the sound of family tragedy.
I was stunned—
   and fell back fainting into my ladies' arms.
But tell me everything however bad;
   I am no stranger to the voice of sorrow.

MESSENGER

Dear Mistress, I was there.
I shall not try to glaze the truth;
   for where is there comfort in a lie,
   so soon found out? The truth is always best
In attendance on your Lord,
   I took him deep into the plain
   where Polyneices lay
   abandoned still—all mauled by dogs.
And there with humble hearts
   we prayed to Hecate, goddess of the Great Divide.
   to Hades too, and begged their clemency.
Then we sprinkled him with holy water,
   lopped fresh branches down
   and laid him on a funeral pyre
   to burn away his poor remains.
Lastly, we heaped a monument to him,
   a mound of his native earth, then turned away
   to unseal the vault in which there lay
   a virgin waiting on a bed of stone
      for her bridegroom—Death.

And one of us, ahead,
   heard a wail of deep despair
   echoing from that hideous place of honeymoon.
He hurried back and told the King,
   who then drew near
   and seemed to recognize those hollow sounds.
He gave a bleat of fear:
"Oh, are my heart's forebodings true?
I cannot bear to tread this path.

My son's voice strikes my ears.
Hurry, hurry, servants, to the tomb,
And through those stones once pried away peer down
    into that cadaverous gap
    and tell me if it's Haemon's voice.
Oh, tell me I am heavenly deceived!"

His panic sent us flying to the cave,
    and in the farthest corner we could see her
    hanging with a noose of linen round her neck,
    and leaning on her,
    hugging his cold lover lost to Hades,
    Haemon, bridegroom, broken,
    cursed the father who had robbed him,
    pouring out his tears of sorrow.

A groan agonized and loud—
    broke from Creon when he saw him.
"You poor misguided boy!" he sobbed,
    staggering forward,
    "What have you done? What were you thinking of?
And now, come to me, my son. Your father begs you."
But the boy glared at him with flaming eyes,
    spat for answer in his face,
    and drawing a double-hilted sword,
    lunged but missed
    as his father stepped aside and ran.
Then, the wretched lad,
    convulsed with self-hatred and despair,
    pressed against that sword and drove it home,
    halfway up the hilt into his side.
And conscious still but failing, limply folded
    Antigone close into his arms—
Choking blood in crimson jets upon her waxen face.
Corpse wrapped in love with corpse he lies,
    married not in life but Hades:
Lesson to the world that inhumane designs
Wreak a havoc immeasurably inhumane.

[EURYDICE *is seen moving like a sleepwalker into the palace*]

LEADER

What does her exit mean?
The Queen has gone without a word of comfort or of
sorrow.

MESSENGER

I am troubled too. And yet I hope
the reason is she shrinks from public sorrow for her son,
And goes into the house to lead her ladies
in the family dirge.
She will not be unwise. She is discreet.

LEADER

You may be right, but I do not trust
extremes of silence or of grief.

MESSENGER

Let me go into the house and see.
Extremes of silence, as you say, are sinister.
Her heart is broken and can hide
some sinister design.

[*As the* MESSENGER *hurries into the palace through a side
door, the great doors open and a procession carrying the
dead body of* HAEMON *on a bier approaches, with* CREON
staggering behind]

CHORUS

Look, the King himself draws near, his load
in a kind of muteness crying out his sorrow
(Dare we say it?) from a madness of misdoing
started by himself and by no other.

CHORAL DIALOGUE

Strophe I

CREON

Purblind sin of mine!
There is no absolution
For perversity that dragged
A son to death:
Murdered son, father murdering.
Son, my son, cut down dead!
New life that's disappeared
And by no youthful foolishness
But by my folly.

CHORUS

Late, too late, your reason reasons right!

Strophe II

CREON

Yes, taught by bitterness.
Some god has cast his spell,
Has hit me hard from heaven,
Let my cruelty grow rank;
Has slashed me down, my joys
Trodden in the earth.
Man, man, oh how you suffer!

[*Enter the* MESSENGER]

MESSENGER

Sire, you are laden,
You the author loading:
Half your sorrow in your hands,
The other half still in your house
Soon to be unhidden.

CREON

What half horror coming?

MESSENGER

Your queen is dead:
Mother for her son;
The suicidal thrust:
Dead for whom she lived.

Antistrophe I

CREON

Oh, Death, pitiless receiver!
Kill me? Will you kill me?
Your mercy dwindles does it?
Must you bring me words
That crush me utterly.
I was dead and still you kill me.
Slaughter was piled high,
Ah then, do not tell me
You come to pile it higher:
A son dead, then a wife.

CHORUS

Look! Everything is open to full view.

[*The scene suddenly opens by a movement of the ekkuklema* to reveal* EURYDICE *lying dead, surrounded by her attendants*]

Antistrophe II

CREON

Oh, oh! A second deathblow.
Fate, my bitter cup

---

*The ekkuklema was a theatrical machine which could open up the stage to an inner scene: frequently a murder or a suicide.

Should have no second brimming,
Yet the sight I see laid out
Compels a second sorrow:
My son just lifted up
A corpse, and now a corpse his mother.

MESSENGER

Her heart was shattered
And her hand drove keen the dagger.
At the altar there she fell
And darkness swamped her drooping eyes
As with cries she sobbed her sorrow
For her hero son Megareus—
Long since nobly dead—
And for this son her other,
Mingling with her dying gasp
Curses on you—killer.

Strophe III

CREON

My heart is sick with dread.
Will no one lance a two-edged sword
Through this bleeding seat of sorrow?

MESSENGER

She charged you, yes,
With both their deaths—
This lifeless thing
As double filicidal killer!

CREON

Tell me, how did she go?

MESSENGER

Self-stabbed to the heart;
Her son's death ringing
New dirges in her head.

Strophe IV

CREON

I killed her, I
Can own no alibi:
The guilt is wholly mine.
Take me quickly, servants,
Take me quickly hence.
Let this nothing be forgotten.

CHORUS

Good advice, at last,
If anything be good
In so much bad.
Such evils need quick riddance.

Antistrophe III

CREON

Oh, let it come! Let it break!
My last and golden day:
The best, the last, the worst
To rob me of tomorrow.

LEADER

Tomorrow is tomorrow
And we must mind today.

CREON

All my prayers are that:
The prayer of my desires.

LEADER

Your prayers are done.
Man cannot flatter Fate,
And punishments must come.

Antistrophe IV

CREON

Then lead me please away,
A rash weak foolish man,
A man of sorrows,
Who killed you, son, so blindly
And you my wife—so blind.
Where can I look?
Where hope for help,
When everything I touch is lost
And death has leapt upon my life?

CHORUS

Where wisdom is, there happiness will crown
A piety that nothing will corrode.
But high and mighty words and ways
Are flogged to humbleness, till age,
Beaten to its knees, at last is wise.

Appendix

PRODUCTION AND ACTING

There are two main dangers in the production of a Greek play: one is to overplay the dignity; the other is not to be aware of that dignity at all. The first becomes a desperate and futile endeavor to recapture the externals of the Greek theater. It is arty and self-conscious and, in battening on period effects (we are being Greeks, boys and girls—is my mask on straight?), destroys the very humanity and timelessness it seeks to promote. The second, confusing the Greek idealization and simplification of human nature with unreality, and seeking to redress the balance, tries to turn the heroic figures of Aeschylus, Sophocles and Euripides into everyday nonentities. It attempts the prosaic, trivial, chatty, and obliterates the heights and depths of tragedy.

These are the two chief false principles. Occasionally they are blended and a third type of mistake is hatched, inheriting the artiness of one parent and the lack of restraint of the other. Professor J. T. Sheppard, the great Sophoclean scholar, well describes it in a production of *Oedipus the King* which he had the discomfort of witnessing: ". . . [the] actors, not altogether, I suspect, of their own free will, raged and fumed and ranted, rushing hither and thither with a violence of gesticulation which, in spite of all their effort, was eclipsed and rendered insignificant by the yet more violent rushes, screams, and contortions of a quite gratuitous crowd." (Introduction to *The Oedipus Tyrannus of Sophocles*, Cambridge, 1920.)

What then is the enlightened producer to aim for? Let him first of all remember that these plays were performed before enormous audiences, perhaps up to 30,000

253

people. Masks, costumes, spectacles, and the whole style of production (whatever its sacred origins) were designed for long-distance effect*: a purpose that no longer exists in our smaller and more intimate theater.

Secondly, this vast audience did not consist predominantly of sophisticated city dwellers but of honest-to-goodness people coming in from the country—many of them farmers and perhaps even (we cannot be certain) slaves. The point is that it was not a highbrow audience, even if it understood better than any modern audience the cultural framework of its own myths. It was not at all the kind of audience that came for culture or would tolerate any "art for art's sake." These people came to be thrilled and moved to tears. All the external apparatus of the Greek stage—song, dance, mime, masks and spectacle—was simply a means to creating a vivid arena wherein the great human emotions could be worked out in public. In some two thousand four hundred years these emotions have not changed. Only the external circumstances have changed. Oedipus, Jocasta, and Antigone were first of all human beings. The heart of Sophocles which beat to their passions was first of all a human heart—only incidentally Greek and of the fifth century B.C.

Thirdly, let both producer and actor remember that it is only through his words—by their very choice and sound—that Sophocles the poet achieves his power to move us. It is through the beauty, restraint, perfect adaptation of every tone and emphasis of the language to each situation, that he is able to sink us deeply into the pathos of his characters. Assuming that the translator has done his best to capture something of the original word-magic, let those words be heard. It is absolutely necessary that the poetry be read as poetry and not given a prose pointing. It is absolutely necessary that the lines are not deprived of their rich embodiment of rhythm and cadence. The poet has already done the work of

*Masks not merely typed a character's predominant expression, but also helped to project the actor's voice (though this second reason is now somewhat discredited).

establishing the necessary tension and dramatic force. No amount of "acting" can be a substitute for it. Let the voice be measured but natural; never "tharsonic," that blend of stage and pulpit which some actors affect when they come to poetry. If the lines are enunciated clearly and rhythmically, if the acting follows the poetry and is not imposed upon it, then the result will tend to be great acting. It will be the transparent window through which the characters—created by the words—are sincerely seen; idealistically human yet never falsely intimate.

As to the Chorus, let the producer keep in mind its purpose: to underline, develop, and if possible increase, the suspense built up by the dialogue. Certainly there can be music, mime, and dance, provided all this does not detract from the intelligibility of the words. The music should tend to build up background rather than to lead. It can be an ally to the force of the poetry if used sensitively and not as an end in itself. Woodwind and percussion instruments—flute and soft drum—would seem to be the most natural accompaniment to the Greek movement. They can be used to usher in and to usher out the main characters. The Sophoclean chorus numbered fifteen, but it can be raised to almost any number or lowered to as few as five. It is better for the chorus to speak its lines severally than to chant them in unison: though there may be occasions when a group answers a group.

The scenery should be simple and not distract the viewer's imagination by striving for realism. A drop curtain may be helpful, though the Greeks did not use one. An interval almost certainly destroys the accumulated tension. If masks are used they should not be replicas of the Greek mask, which was much larger than life.

These then are the principles. There are few rules, if many possibilities. Only that production of a Greek play will be valid which puts the human emotions first and enables the spectator to feel with and for its subjects. Let producer and actor resist the two falsifying temptations: the purely mundane, which can never be heroic, and the overstylized, which can never be human.

NOTES

(1) Note on Meter

The meter throughout the dialogue of this rendering of the Theban Plays is iambic, as it is in Sophocles. If to anyone's eye it reads too unvaryingly I can only counsel him to read it aloud, keeping to the natural stresses of the words. Dramatic speech automatically tends to create its own background of counterpoint rhythms. Indeed, the danger on the stage is not that poetry should sound monotonous but that it should not sound at all. Sophocles himself never loses his hold on an unmistakable "beat" which should not be lost in the English even though English prosody is "qualitative" rather than "quantitative." In either language it is the beauty of the measure itself that contributes to the depth, loftiness and intensity of the drama.

In my original translation of the Oedipus Plays, published by New American Library in 1958, I wrote: "In the *Antigone* I keep to a more or less traditional blank versification, but in the other two plays I have made the attempt to tauten the metrical value of dramatic speech while at the same time rendering it more elastic and capacious. In *Oedipus the King* I have adopted a prosodical device which helps the line to follow the sense of the words more than it does in ordinary iambic pentameter. The lines lengthen and shorten as the need may be, but whether they stretch into hexameters or shrink into trimeters the overall count of a passage remains iambic pentameter. I have called it "Compensated Pentameter." In *Oedipus at Colonus*, to match by some kind of prosodical analogy this last and supreme mastery of Sophocles over human speech, I have done away with even compensation and embark on a completely free-wheeling iambic measure which I think (and hope) is proof against all misreading."

Since that time, I have come to the conclusion that this last solution is the best, and it is what I adhere to in this new rendition in all three plays. The free-wheeling iambic measure seems to me to get nearest to that amazing wedding in the Greek of formality to spontaneity and fluidity.

There is one other observation I should like to make. In the Choruses and Choral Dialogues I have mostly returned to the traditional usage of beginning each line with a capital rather than following the present practice of using lower case. My motive is to discourage readers (especially actors) from treating verse, even when dialogue, as ordinary expository prose. I make no apologies for this decision. We live in an age when lack of faith (or is it courage?) in the power of poetry to communicate before and beyond the point at which it enters the cerebrum, drives readers to make verse look and sound like prose as soon as possible.

(2) Note on *Oedipus the King*

The power of *Oedipus the King* is cumulative. It opens slowly, weightily, and rises to a flood of emotion that nothing can stop. This initial solemnity—at times almost a stiffness—I have been at pains to keep in the English. It is a formal and hieratic quality and lasts till about line 86, the first exit of OEDIPUS. However, it must not be assumed that this "grand manner" of utterance casts aside the already perceptible elements of pity, pathos, irony, fear, and suffering which come to such full fruition later.

(3) Note on Creon

It must not be thought that the character of CREON in *Oedipus the King* corresponds exactly to the CREON in the other two plays. The Theban Plays were not written at the same time nor conceived originally as a strict unity.

(4) Note on the Appearance of the Greek Script

For those who are interested, here are the first six lines of the *Antigone* written out in Greek lower case. If they are written out in capitals (as Greek often was) they will look like the lines at the beginning of this book. It is the same passage.

＊Ω κοινὸν αὐτάδελφον ᾽Ισμήνης κάρα
ἆρ᾽ ἆσθ᾽ ὅτι Ζεὺς τῶν ἀπ᾽ Οἰδίπου κακῶν
ὁποῖον οὐχὶ νῷν ἔτι ζώσαιν τελεῖ,
οὐδὲν γὰρ οὔτ᾽ ἀλγεινὸν οὔτ᾽ ἄτης ἄτερ
οὔτ᾽ αἰσχρὸν οὔτ᾽ ἄτιμόν ἐσθ᾽ ὁποῖον οὐ
τῶν σῶν τε καμῶν οὐκ ὄπώπ᾽ ἐγὼ κακῶν.

(5) Note on the Texts

The texts I have followed have in the main been those of Lewis Campbell, Oxford, 1879, and Richard Jebb, Cambridge, 1889–93. I support Campbell as against Jebb in not excising lines 904–12 of the *Antigone*. These lines seem to me to throw important light on ANTIGONE's character and motives.

(6) Notes on the Handling of the Chorus

In general, let the director never forget that the Chorus must be elevated to an art convincing in its own right. This means that the Chorus must be worth watching and listening to almost regardless of the rest of the play. Though commenting on, condensing, and recording the action of the drama, the Chorus should transcend it, lift it to a new plane of experience—the lyrical. This is accomplished only by being poetically different from the realism (naturalism) of each episode. The verses must be treated as pure poetry—that is, as a vehicle of illumination that communicates before, or at least beyond the point at which it is understood. The important question is not so much whether the Choruses are intelligible, as whether they sweep the audience off its feet the way music and dance can. The following suggestions on how to direct a Chorus may be helpful. They embody some of the stratagems I would employ if I were staging a Greek play.

(a) Make the size of the Chorus as large as is compatible with the size of the stage, remembering that twelve people are generally more impressive than three.

(b) Have the Chorus trained in dance and mime and let the dancing be more or less continuous throughout the play, though obviously more restrained during the dialogue parts of the episodes.

(c) Rarely allow the Chorus to speak directly (except of course where it takes part in the dialogue). Instead, have the words coming "voice-over" their movements, either by direct voice beyond the stage or prerecorded, or both: in all cases amplified and made larger than life. (The reason I am disinclined to let the Chorus speak is that I have found that performers generally appear overly self-conscious when forced to dance, sing, mime, and recite at the same time.)

(d) For this same reason, recitation in unison is difficult to bring off convincingly, and I prefer the single amplified voice. Of course, there may be occasions where voices in unison may be attempted, as well as other sonic experiments. For instance, after a first straight hearing, the words can be fragmented into various patterns of repetition, cross-cutting, overlapping, truncation, and so on. They can echo liturgical prayers, litanies, chants—the English perhaps played off against the sound of classical Greek—or even turned into wounded animal sounds. Here it would be wise to call in the assistance of an imaginative musical director who knows all the tricks of electronic recording. Another inventive approach would be to have the actions of the Chorus turned into living tableaux during the voice-overs. These tableaux can be sometimes moving, sometimes still—frozen into certain attitudes. Remember always that the aim is to make the Chorus—both in sound and sight—breathtaking.

(e) As to the straight recitation of the Chorus verses,

they should be beaten out rhythmically with little attempt to make them sound "natural." The design of the poetry must be allowed to appear, and not turned into prose. For instance, when the sense of the words requires the end of one line to be run into the next, let the reciter create the illusion of doing this, but he must not actually do it. The ear must not be cheated of the incantatory effect of the line as a musical unit.

(f) The choice of music is crucial. There should be music throughout the play, introducing scenes, repeating themes, coming in and out of both the dialogue and the choruses. Care must be taken, however, that the words always be given first place. Never should the audience have to strain to hear the words above the music. As to instruments, I favor drum, flute, and lute (perhaps guitar and harp) as coming nearest to the Greek timbal, flageolet, and lyre.

(g) In general, let the director remember that a Greek play stands or falls by the quality of the Chorus. Too often one gets the impression that the embarrassed director, at his wit's end, wants to get the Chorus out of the way as soon as possible. Sometimes it seems the Chorus is being twisted into part of the dialogue. No, the Chorus must exist for its own sake and for the arresting beauty of its own design. Besides being esthetically irresistible the Chorus has the function of relieving the audience of dramatic tension (building after each episode) and introducing a new tension which is lyric and hits below the belt—that is, below the level of the conscious mind.

GLOSSARY OF CLASSICAL NAMES

Abae: An ancient town in the country of Phocis (northern Greece) which was famous for its temple and oracle of Apollo.

Acheron: A river of the lower world, around which the souls of the dead were said to hover.

Aidoneus: Another name for Hades—god of the Nether World.

Amphion: With his twin brother Zethus, Amphion marched against Thebes, killed Lycus the King (their cast-off mother's husband) and Dirce, who had become Lycus's wife. They tied Dirce to a bull which dragged her about until she was dead, then they threw her body into a fountain—hence "Dirce's Fountain." Hermes gave Amphion a lyre on which he played with such magic skill that the stones moved of their own accord and formed a great wall around Thebes.

Amphitrite: Wife of the god Poseidon and goddess of the sea. She was the mother of Triton.

Aphrodite: Goddess of love and beauty. The Roman Venus.

Apollo: The son of Zeus and Leto. He was the god of prophecy, of help and reward, and of punishment. He had more influence upon the Greeks than any other one god.

Areopagus: Criminal court of Athens—so called because it sat on the Hill of Ares, west of the Acropolis.

Ares: Bloodthirsty god of war. Roman Mars.

Argos: A city-state in the Peloponnesus. Also, a rival to Sparta.

Artemis: Twin sister of Apollo and goddess of the moon and of the hunt. She sent plagues and sudden deaths (especially to women), but she also cured and alleviated sufferings. She is the Roman Diana.

Athena: Or Athene—the Roman Minerva. Daughter of Zeus and Metis (Zeus swallowed her mother before her birth and Athena sprang from his head—dressed in full armor and shouting a mighty war cry). **Goddess of power and wisdom,** Athena was the preserver of the state and maintained law and order. She is said to have created the olive tree and invented the plow.

Attica: A division of Greece in which Athens was the principal city.

Bacchus: Earlier called Dionysus. Greek and Roman god of wine and revelry.

Bacchanal: Religious revelry centered around the god Bacchus.

Bacchae: Priestesses of Dionysus who by wine and mad enthusiasm worked themselves to a frenzy at the Dionysiac festivals.

Boreas: God of the North Wind. In the Persian War he helped the Athenians by destroying the ships of the barbarians.

Cadmus: Son of Agenor, king of Phoenicia, and also the brother of Europa. He founded Thebes by killing a dragon sacred to Ares and then on the advice of Athena sowing its teeth. Armed men sprang up from the ground who fought and killed one another till only five remained. These five then helped Cadmus to build the city of Thebes.

Castalia: A fountain on Mount Parnassus sacred to Apollo.

Cephisus: The largest stream in Attica.

Cerberus: The three-headed dog which guarded the entrance of Hades Halls.

Cithaeron: A lofty mountain range separating Boeotia from Megaris and Attica. It was sacred to Dionysus.

Corybantes: The attendants of the Phrygian goddess Cybele, who followed her through the night with dancing and revelry.

Cronus: Youngest of the Titans—son of Uranus (heaven) and Ge or Gaea (earth). He was father, by Rhea, of Hestia, Demeter, Hera, Hades, Poseidon, and Zeus. He ousted Uranus from divine supremacy and in turn was dethroned by Zeus. He is the Roman Saturn.

Cyllene: The highest mountain in the Peloponnesus.

Danaë: She was locked in a brazen tower by her father

because an oracle said her son would grow to kill its grandfather. In her tower Zeus visited her in a shower of gold, and thus impregnated she gave birth to Perseus—who years later accidentally killed his grandfather with a discus.

Daulia: An ancient town in Phocis.

Delos: The smallest of the Cyclades islands. As it was the birthplace of Apollo and Artemis, Delos became the holy seat of the worship of Apollo and the site of a famous temple.

Delphi: A small town in Phocis, but the most celebrated in Greece because of its oracle of Apollo.

Demeter: Sister of Zeus, goddess of earth, protectress of agriculture and all the fruits of the earth. She became identified with the Roman Ceres.

Dionysus: God of wine and the god of tragic art and protector of the theater. The Roman Bacchus.

Dirce: See Amphion.

Dragon's Seed: The armed men that sprang up from the teeth of the dragon which Cadmus slew. They fought and killed one another except five, who became the ancestors of the Thebans.

Dryads: Nymphs of the woods (female divinities of the lower order).

Dryas: Father of the Thracian king, Lycurgus.

Edonia: A part of Thrace where the people were celebrated for their orgiastic worship of Bacchus.

Eleusis: A town of Attica, northwest of Athens, which had a magnificent temple of Demeter, and gave its name to the great festival and mysteries of the Eleusinia, which were celebrated in honor of Persephone and Demeter.

Erectheus: (Erichthonius)—son of Hephaestus. Athena reared him without the other gods' knowing. He became king of Athens and is said to have introduced the worship of Athena there.

Eumenides: The "Kindly Ones" (which is a euphemism for the Furies or Erinyes, dreaded daughters of Earth and Night). They were usually represented as winged maidens with serpents entwined in their hair and blood dripping from their eyes. They dwelt in the depths of

Tartarus. They punished humans both in this world and after death—usually for disobedience toward parents, disrespect of old age, perjury, murder, violation of laws of hospitality, and improper conduct toward suppliants.

Euxine: The Black Sea.

Furies: See Eumenides.

Hades: See Aidoneus.

Helicon: Range of mountains in Boeotia which are covered in snow most of the year. They were sacred to Apollo and the Muses. From Helicon sprang the famous fountains of the Muses.

Helios: God of the sun who sees and hears everything.

Hephaestus: God of fire and the forge, who made Achilles' shield. Son of Zeus and Hera. The Roman Vulcan.

Hermes: The Roman Mercury. Usually depicted wearing winged shoes and hat and carrying the caduceus in his hand. He was the herald and messenger of the gods and also invented the lyre. He conducted the shades of the dead from the upper to the lower world.

Iacchus: The solemn name of Bacchus in the Eleusinian mysteries.

Io: Beloved by Zeus and hated by Hera, who turned her into a heifer. Hera tormented her with a gadfly. In a constant state of frenzy, she fled from land to land until she at last found rest on the banks of the Nile and returned to her original form.

Ismenus: A small river in Boeotia, the stream Dirce flowed into.

Ister: The river Danube, flowing to the Black Sea through the land of the Scythians.

Isthmian: The Isthmian games were held once a year on the Isthmus of Corinth.

Lyceus: A surname of Apollo, who was worshipped in Lycia, a small district in South Asia Minor.

Maenads: Another name for the Bacchantes, meaning "to be mad," because they were frenzied in their worship of Bacchus.

Mars: Roman name for Ares, god of war.

Megareus: A son of Eurydice, wife of Creon.

Mercury: Roman name for Hermes.

Nemesis: The goddess who measured out happiness and misery, visiting suffering and losses on those who were too fortunate. She became known as the divinity who punished the criminal.

Niobe: The daughter of Tantalus and wife of Amphion, king of Thebes. She boasted of the number of her children, thus annoying Apollo and Artemis, who slew all her children. Zeus turned the weeping mother into a stone on Mount Sipylus in Lydia, which even during the summer always shed tears.

Nymphs: Minor goddesses of nature, haunting rivers (Naiads), woods and trees (Dryads and Hamadryads), mountains (Oreads), and seas (Nereids).

Nyssa: The legendary scene of the nurture of Dionysus. It came to mean several places sacred to Dionysus.

Oea: A deme (small district) in Attica belonging to the Oenean tribe.

Olympus: The highest of the range of mountains separating Macedonia and Thessaly. It was the home of Zeus and all his dynasty.

Pallas: A surname of Athena.

Pan: A son of Hermes. The god of shepherds and flocks. He loved music and invented the syrinx or shepherd's flute. He led the nymphs in dance, but, as he had the legs and horns of a goat and dwelt in the forests, travelers were frightened of him.

Parnassus: A mountain range in southern Greece: usually signifying the highest part, which is a few miles north of Delphi. It was the seat of Apollo and the Muses, and sacred to Dionysus.

Peiritheus: A hero in Attic history who gave his name to a deme (one of the hundred townships into which Attica was divided).

Peloponnesus: Southern peninsula of Greece, connected with Hellas by the isthmus of Corinth. It contained the powerful city-states of Sparta and Argos.

Pelops: Meaning the Peloponnesus, which was named after Pelops, son of Tantalus, who came to Elis and brought with him such riches that the whole peninsula was named for him.

Persephone: Daughter of Zeus and Demeter and wife of Hades, therefore Queen of the Dead. The Roman Proserpine.

Phasis: A river of Colchis in Asia Minor from whose banks the pheasant is said to have come.

Phineus: Who blinded his own sons because of alleged treachery. The gods punished him in turn with blindness and sent the Harpies to torment him. The sons of Boreas eventually freed him from the monsters.

Phoebus: "Bright" or "Pure"—an epithet of Apollo.

Phrygia: A country in Asia Minor, probably settled by Thracians.

Pluto: Another name for Hades—used as euphemism by those who were frightened to mention Hades.

Poseidon: God of the Mediterranean. Brother of Zeus and Hades, who rode his chariot over the waves and lived in a palace in the depths of the sea. The Roman Neptune.

Prometheus: A god who stole fire from heaven and taught the mortals its use, and many arts. He was chained to a rock and submitted to the perpetual torture of an eagle's eating away his liver (and Zeus's healing it each night so that the eagle could begin again). Hercules eventually freed him.

Pythia: A priestess of Delphi, who, after exhaling the intoxicating vapors which rose from the ground in the center of the temple, uttered the revelations of Apollo.

Pytho: The ancient name of Delphi.

Rhea: Mother of Zeus, Poseidon, Hades, Hera, Demeter, Hestia. "Mother of the Gods," who was wildly and often orgiastically worshiped through the whole of Greece.

Sardis: An ancient city of Asia Minor which contained the palace and the rich treasury of the Lydian kings.

Semele: The daughter of Theban Cadmus who was beloved by Zeus. Jealous Hera tricked her into asking Zeus to visit her as god of thunder. He warned Semele of the danger but nevertheless complied. She was killed by lightning but Zeus saved her child, Dionysus, whom she had just conceived by Zeus (as thunder). Dionysus later carried her from the underworld to Olympus and she became immortal.

Sipylus: See Niobe.

Sphinx: "The Strangler," a winged monster with a lion's body and the head and breasts of a woman. She took up her station on a rock outside Thebes and proposed a riddle to every passerby, strangling those who could not answer. When Oedipus solved the riddle she flung herself from her rock and perished.

Tantalus: A wealthy, worldly king, and son of Zeus. After his death Zeus punished him in the underworld by eternal thirst and hunger. He placed him in a lake, which receded from him each time he tried to drink, and beneath branches of fruit which Tantalus could never quite reach.

Tartarus: A name synonymous with Hades. Also a place as far below Hades as Heaven is above the earth.

Thebes: The chief city of Boeotia; said to have been founded by the hero Cadmus. The walls of the city were built by Amphion and his brother Zethus. Legend had it that when Amphion played his lyre, the stones themselves moved into place to form the wall.

Thoricus: A hero in Attic history who gave his name to a deme (one of the hundred townships into which Attica was divided).

Thrace: A city-state in northern Greece which was inhabited by rapacious and warlike people.

Titans: Giant deities, the primordial children of Heaven and Earth, who were overthrown and succeeded by Zeus and the Olympian gods.

Zeus: The Roman Jupiter: greatest, most powerful, and ruler of all the Olympian gods. The husband of Hera, the Roman Juno.

Acknowledgments

In my original rendition of the Oedipus Plays, I made grateful acknowledgment to the following professors and associate professors for their criticism and suggestions:

Mr. Bernard N. W. Knox of Yale University
Mr. Martin Ostwald of Columbia University
Miss Helen Bacon of Smith College
Mr. John A. Moore of Amherst College.

I also thanked the trustees of the Bollingen Foundation for the award that enabled me to translate the *Oedipus at Colonus* on the island of Nevis in the West Indies.

Lastly, in this new and revised version, I want to thank my percipient editor at Dutton Signet, Ms. Rosemary Ahern.